# I DON'T KNOW
# WHY SHE BOTHERS

# GUILT-FREE
## MOTHERHOOD
### for Thoroughly
### Modern Women

## DAISY WAUGH

PHOENIX

A PHOENIX PAPERBACK

First published in Great Britain in 2013
by Weidenfeld & Nicolson
This edition published in 2014
by Phoenix,
an imprint of Orion Books Ltd,
Orion House, 5 Upper St Martin's Lane,
London WC2H 9EA

An Hachette UK Company

1 3 5 7 9 10 8 6 4 2

A CIP catalogue record for this book
is available from the British Library.

ISBN: 978-1-7802-2450-3

Typeset by Input Data Services Ltd, Bridgwater, Somerset

Printed and bound by CPI Group (UK) Ltd, Croydon, CR0 4YY

The Orion Publishing Group's policy is to use papers that
are natural, renewable and recyclable products and
made from wood grown in sustainable forests. The logging
and manufacturing processes are expected to conform to
the environmental regulations of the country of origin.

www.orionbooks.co.uk

Daisy Waugh has written as an agony aunt, restaurant critic, celebrity interviewer, property correspondent and a lifestyle columnist from London, the country and Hollywood. She writes historical novels, most recently *Melting the Snow on Hester Street*. She has three children and lives in London.

Twitter: @dldwaugh   Website: daisywaugh.co.uk

# CONTENTS

# PART 1

# MOTHERHOOD

*(Losing The Halo)*

## Recent Studies Have Shown ...

*Researchers have found that children born to older mothers are better at language and face fewer social and emotional problems, compared with children born to young mothers.*

Recent studies show children of older mothers have a higher risk of autism.

*Recent studies have shown late development, poor verbal skills and lower test scores in children whose mothers returned to work during the very early months of their babies' lives.*

Researchers have found that mothers who are over-involved or overprotective during the early stages of a child's development can increase the risk of their child developing problems with anxiety later in life.

*Experiments have shown that kids who watch age-appropriate educational programmes show immediate improvements in their abilities to recall information and to solve the sorts of problems modelled in the shows.*

Studies show that watching television may hamper the development of children's prefrontal cortex – the area of the brain responsible for planning, organising and sequencing behaviour affecting self-control, moral judgement and attention.

*Recent studies have shown that babies who are solely breast-fed for the first six months of life are at a greater risk of developing nut allergies.*

Recent studies show that infants who are breast-fed are less likely to suffer from ear infections.

*New research shows that 'housewives' are more likely to be obese than those who juggle children, a steady relationship and a pay cheque.*

New research reveals working mums face a higher risk of heart disease than other women.

*Recent studies have shown that infants who were breast-fed cry more, smile and laugh less, and are harder to soothe and get off to sleep than their formula-fed counterparts.*

Recent studies have shown that alcohol is actually less addictive than KFC's chicken.

... It's tempting when trying to make a point (especially an argumentative one: viz., most of what follows), to have a quick trawl through Google in search of a study or statistic to back it up. Look hard enough and there will almost certainly be one. And although studies per se are clearly a Very Good Thing, when being used to illustrate quite a strong a point of view, they are probably best taken with a pinch of salt. The above list of beguiling but contradictory 'information' took me about half an hour to cobble together, while I was waiting for a yoga class to begin.

There are lies, damn lies – and there is a quick trawl through Google for some slick-sounding studies to back them up. I am going to resist the temptation to bamboozle us all with studies (unless I think they're funny) and kick off with a nice little questionnaire instead. Pencils at the ready, laydies! Here comes the science bit.

## What Type Of Mum Are YOU?

Look carefully at the statements on the following page, and rate them according to how strongly you agree or disagree. (Remember: there are no 'Correct Answers'. Not all mums are the same!)

By using the box, you can 'calculate' your score. First, add up your 'Correct Answers'. (Don't panic! It's actually a lot simpler than it sounds.) Finally, we'll tell you what type of Mummy you *really* are. Alpha or Yummy? Selfish or Super? Mega-Nice or Mega-Evil? Come on girls! 'Fess up!

**I love my kids!**

AGREE STRONGLY! ☺/STRONGLY DISAGREE! ☹

---

**I really love my kids!**

AGREE STRONGLY! ☺ /STRONGLY DISAGREE! ☹

---

**I really, *really* love my kids!**

AGREE STRONGLY! ☺/STRONGLY DISAGREE! ☹

---

*OKAY, HOW DID YOU DO?*

> **MOSTLY 'AGREE STRONGLY! ☺'S**
>
> Congratulations, Mum! You're doin' GREAT!
>
> **MOSTLY 'STRONGLY DISAGREE! ☹'S**
>
> Oops! Sounds like you may be struggling with 'Being A Mum'! You might want to consider taking a PARENTING COURSE.
>
> PARENTING COURSES aren't as scary as they sound! They're inexpensive and most mums agree, they can be a whole lot of fun, too! Plus they're a super way to meet other 'Struggling Mums' just like you!
>
>  Ask your GP for a leaflet!

## Congratulations, Mum! You're Doin' GREAT!

Yeah. Thanks.

So I was at a working lunch not so long ago, sitting at a long dining table, surrounded by clever, serious men. It was an unusual party because in a roomful of twenty or more, only three of us were women: an Estonian intern, amazingly pretty, in her early twenties, who didn't seem to speak any English; an older woman, gentle and unassuming; and the secretary to the man who was hosting the lunch. And me. Out of my depth, outnumbered. And a bit restless. But the food was good, and it made a change from writing.

One of the guests was an expert on welfare reform. (This story gets better.) He was a highly respected gentleman, with a mean mouth, I noticed, but a good suit; and he was advising this government, as he had the last, on sundry initiatives related to benefit-dependent single mothers. And maybe – who knows? – some of his illiberal-sounding initiatives might indeed prove helpful one day. But in my heart I doubted it, if only because of the scorn-filled tone he used when discussing them. He had statistics – plenty of them – and an unshakeable confidence in his own rectitude; and a noticeable dislike for the people he proclaimed himself so keen to help.

In any case – call it sentimental (I'm sure he would) – but it seemed to me that, statistics or no statistics, any child-rearing initiative devised by gentlemen with mean mouths and smart suits, enjoying extravagant weekday luncheons in

Mayfair dining rooms where there aren't enough women present, was unlikely to bring much wisdom or kindness to the forum.

The main gist of his intended reform was faintly reminiscent of that creepy Tom Cruise film, *Minority Report*, in which, thanks to a brilliant fortune-telling computer, government officers could incarcerate villains for 'pre-crimes' before they'd had a chance to think of committing them. The thin-lipped man wanted to send 'parental instruction officers' – I'm not sure what name he had devised for them – into the homes of young, single mothers who looked as though they might yet prove unfit for the difficult task ahead.

These teenage girls, the gentlemen around me agreed, simply hadn't the faintest idea what was required of them, and they needed to be told.

Quite quickly, the conversation took what I felt was a nasty turn; and if I'd known I was going to write about it later, I would have made notes. At the time, I sat as politely as I could while the steam began to whistle inside my ears. Mr Thin Lips delivered his statistics and anecdotes with a sneering viciousness, and the clever men of Mayfair – of all political persuasions, I should add – nodded and sighed, and rolled their eyes at the desperate state of the masses, until the plates were cleared for pudding.

*Some of these little children*, we were told, arrived at school having been so horribly neglected by their so-called 'mothers' that they couldn't recognise their own names. They couldn't dress themselves. They weren't potty-trained ... They'd never laid eyes on a 'book' ... Many of them couldn't even speak properly ... The single skill guaranteed to every one of them, it seemed, was the ability to open a family-size pack of crisps.

*What these mothers needed ... What these irresponsible girls failed to appreciate ... What these selfish, lazy women had to be made to understand ...* The men's conversation seemed to take for granted that there exists an approved and correct way for all humans to raise their human children: free of crisps, and full of books, with matching values, tastes, diets, hygiene and literacy levels for each and every one of us. Unimaginative? Clearly. And diminishing? Well I thought so, yes. We are not all the same. We do not all want the same things. It's what makes each human so valuable and interesting.

God knows, I've no doubt there are some cruel and irresponsible mothers out there, and I've no doubt that in the course of his research, old Thin Lips had encountered more than most. But something in all the gentlemen's tones, how lightly they dismissed these apparently hopeless women, how easily and complacently they judged and damned their maternal efforts, crystallised an irritation which had been bubbling away for years. And I have to say, the anger I felt listening to them sneering and despairing from their easy moral high ground, took me quite by surprise.

So, you know how it is. One minute, you're sitting politely, slightly intimidated, listening to the experts. Next minute, it occurs to you that there might, in fact, be a few naked emperors at the table – still pretty intimidating, certainly, but not for such persuasive reasons. I looked at these men – from one to the next – and I wondered which of them had played what kind of a role in the potty-training of their own wretched toddlers.

More to the point, what was the longest stretch of time spent by any one of these excellent gentlemen, absolutely, utterly and entirely alone with a child of under two years old?

A single morning? A weekend? Maybe even one, whole, long, nightmarish week? Perhaps their wife was in hospital, their mother was dead, they had no sympathetic neighbours, no sisters, no in-laws, no nannies available, no au pairs and no friends ... *But even then* (I thought) they would always have known that such an arrangement was temporary. Some ghastly mismanagement on the part of someone else, probably female, had led them to this unavoidable situation. And it would be okay. Because everyone would feel sorry for them, and laugh indulgently at their incompetent efforts ... And in any case, even a week of solitary potty-training is bearable. For a clever fellow in a suit. If he knows that, come Monday, he'll be safely back at his piss-'n'-puke-free desk. Engaging his brain, and, above all, not feeling guilty about leaving the potty-training and crisp-packet-opening to somebody else.

Anyway, after several long minutes of listening quietly and smiling pleasantly at this VIP luncheon, I began to feel incredibly angry ... so angry that my vision began to zoom in and out of focus.

'You bang on as if these women were barely human!' I burst out, before I had quite noticed I was speaking.

'But you don't seem to realise – the very fact that those crisp-eating children still *exist* by school age is a testament ... [I didn't put it quite as neatly as this.] The mere fact ... [I sort of said] that these children made it as far as primary school at all is testament to their mother's love. You're all sitting around sneering – but do you have the faintest idea how much effort and care is required, simply to keep a baby alive?'

I said something along those lines, and I definitely said the bit about them sitting around sneering – thereby, idiotically, not just declaring war on the usual world-going-to-hell, selfish-mummy orthodoxy, but declaring war on the entire room. I rounded off my passionate speech with a sweetener; an emperor-sized nugget of humour which I thought might help to smooth things over, while also, pretty much, summing up:

'What I'm trying to say is … Maybe a few rotten apples – like Stalin, for example – maybe *Stalin* didn't manage it … but on the whole, in general … I bet *the Russians love their children too* … '

They looked angry and confused. Because very clever gentlemen sometimes just don't get pop references.

'You're coming at the whole matter of motherhood from the wrong angle.' (I tried again.) 'You may not approve of the way they manifest it. Or don't manifest it. You may disapprove of how many crisps they eat. But these women aren't raising children for your benefit and approval. And even if you find it hard to spot any charm in their feral, snot-nosed offspring, *they* can spot it. *They* love their children. Even if *you* can't understand how or why.'


… Actually this book isn't about men. They are the least of our problems. I'm only setting them up as common foe so that the rest of us – the ones actually doing the potty-training, or feeling guilty about employing someone else to do it – can be loosely united, if only in that: yummy mummy, slummy mummy, bummy, cummy, dummy mummy and every scummy 'mummy' in between no matter what we feed our children, how hard we work or don't work, how too old or too young we may be – or how often we read them Shakespeare before bed ... This is a book in defence of 'mummies' everywhere: who are fed up with the constant commentary; the stream of unsolicited, sentimental, impractical and guilt-inducing advice – on something which we might do far more enjoyably (and far better), if left to our own instinctively irritable and lazy – but loving – devices.

Not all mothers love their children, of course. And I pity the infinitesimal few who can't, almost as much as I pity their offspring ... But I should make it clear, I don't speak for them. Only for the rest of us: for that truly vast majority of women, who, in our own imperfect and infinitely varied fashions, in the privacy of our heads and hearts, love our children fiercely and without the smallest shadow of doubt, but who nevertheless sometimes feel the need to go to extravagant and impractical ends to prove it – not to ourselves, nor to our children, but to an ever more neurotically censorious and sentimental outside world.

Modern parenting, like the gentlemen at lunch, disapproves of idiosyncrasy. It requires all of life to be laid flat and bite-sized at the altar of a child's *serenity*. Leaving aside the spirit-sapping assumption that serenity is the be-all-and-end-all of a well-lived life, it fails to take into account the fact that loving mothers and beloved children often want different things from the world, and from each other, too. Some of us like eating crisps and watching *X Factor* together. Others may feel more comfortable drinking soya milk and reading Ovid – in separate rooms. We don't all have to dance to an identical jig. In fact, if I may say so, if we don't feel like it, we don't have to bloody well jig at all.

... And yet ...

As the civilised world continues on its long and laudable trek towards greater tolerance in other forums, the Good Mother prototype seems to have got stuck – or worse – it seems to have regressed, becoming ever more rigid and one-dimensional. To the point where even the smallest aberrations from the simpering, slavish norm can be scowled at. As any pregnant woman who's dared to drink alcohol in a pub – or God forbid, light a cigarette – soon discovers. Such minor lapses in personal, prenatal care (if lapses they are at all) are looked upon now as monstrous crimes, monstrous enough for *total strangers* to feel comfortably within their rights to approach and remonstrate!

We live, for the most part, in an unselfconsciously selfish society. It's the way it is. It's how we've evolved. It's how we've learned to survive. But future mothers are meant to set themselves apart from that, and to forget everything we were taught about the importance of 'self-actualisation' and self-reliance; of 'life being a journey', 'fulfilling our potential', '*Going For It*' ... and so on.

We are supposed to cast all that aside, fix a hurried halo over our heads, and offer ourselves up as nothing more than grateful, glowing livestock.

Hopes and dreams, personal tastes and individual requirements – all the things that raise us above animals and make us human – become, not simply irrelevant, but actually faintly embarrassing. As if their mere existence might somehow undermine not only a mother's gratitude for the gift of giving life, but the magnificence of Mother Love itself.

I started writing a new novel when I was pregnant with my first child. It was a novel that required plenty of research. I lost count of the number of people who smiled knowingly when I talked about it who said to me, 'Well I don't suppose you'll be bothering much with that sort of thing now ...'

How is a woman to respond to that? Without either picking a fight or quietly despairing? I simpered and prayed they were wrong. But lacked the confidence, back then, to say anything at all. (When one of my uncles said it, his wife, my aunt, leant across the table and punched him. For which I will love her for ever.) But we don't all have such excellent aunts.

What we have, for the most part, is repressive sentimentality, a smiling acceptance of female martyrdom, which teeters, at times, beyond martyrdom into a sort of approved, mass-culture masochism.

It's creepy.

And it reaches its creepiest, most perverted climax in the delivery room, where women, for reasons that have never made any sense to me, are encouraged to endure the extraordinary pain of labour without calling on the perfectly safe and incredibly effective painkillers which we all know to be available.

I have three children. During labour for the first (before I knew any better), so pumped up was I, with nerves and hormones and fear of disapproval, I allowed the midwife to negotiate me out of an epidural and into a fucking *birthing pool*. She said I was very lucky one had come free. So I lay in this idiotic tub, naked, frightened – and in agony, while my husband and the midwife stood awkwardly side by side looking down at me.

Painful. Humiliating. Lonely.

But we learn. By Baby Number 3, I knew exactly what I wanted. And though the doctor rolled her eyes and looked queasy, and told me 'only the middle-class women' insisted on epidurals on the NHS (perhaps because only the middle-class women are confident enough to demand them?), the hospital eventually relented.

Better still, I had a husband who travelled, other children to care for, and I was living in a place far away from family and friends. So, I had something called a 'social induction'. In other words, I was given drugs specifically so that the baby was born at a time to fit with my schedule. And – bless that scruffy little hospital – before anyone even gave me the induction drugs, they fitted me up with an epidural. Which meant, reader, a one hundred per cent pain-free delivery, at a time that suited me!

Oh yeah.

The midwife was an older woman: earthy, gossipy and warm.

We chatted up to the last minute. About all sorts of things – her grandchildren and my children, *The Apprentice*, Take That ... At some point our conversation was interrupted by one of those shattering, agonised screams, the like of which you only hear on battlefields (I imagine) and on NHS delivery wards, where they're being stingy with the epidurals. The woman in the room next door, I was told, had 'opted' for a 'natural delivery'.

So natural, her screams made the flimsy walls between our two rooms shake. As the screams faded, and the wretched woman paused for the panting exercises they no doubt told her would help with the next agonising round of contractions, my midwife gave a merry, bosomy chuckle, and shook her head.

'Another natural childbirth,' she laughed. 'I don't know why they bother.'

It's a question I've been asking myself about so many aspects of modern motherhood ever since.

### I Really, Really Love My Kids! ☺

Indeed, I do.

I love my children. I really, really love my children.

The oldest is only 15, so I am guessing the worst may be yet to come, but at time of writing, I can say without hesitation, since the day each one of them was born, my children have been my greatest pride and joy. Funny, independent, individual, warm, spirited, curious, bold, kind, clever, thoughtful – and beautiful; they light up every room they walk into. They light up my life. I love nothing more than spending time with them. And I am daily astonished by my good fortune in being their mother. I love my children.

But you can tie up the sick bag now. I won't continue. And really, I think it's faintly absurd that I should feel the need to say it at all. I love my children. Of course I love my golden, perfect, miraculous children. Who doesn't? It was ever thus. It's how the human race continues.

Trouble is, since women ventured into the world beyond their kitchens, something's gone awry. Hot on the heels of freedom, our guilt came a-knocking. And for some mad reason, we mothers didn't turn our backs on it. On the contrary, we opened the door and *welcomed it in*. We gave it pride of place at the head of our table.

Where once a mother's 'mothering skills' were assumed (and could ever a single phrase exude less natural joy or spontaneity?), now they are scrutinised, measured, judged – and disapproved of. Between us we have allowed the bar to be set so preposterously high, it's impossible not to feel like a failure – no matter what we do or don't do. And it's infuriating to think that we are constantly berating ourselves, constantly straining to *do* more and *prove* more, when we could simply be enjoying what we have – namely relishing our hard-fought independence and freedom, celebrating our good fortune of having been born at such a time, in such place, and wallowing in the joy of our children's company. It's such a waste of potential happiness!

And for all of that, we have only ourselves to blame ...

As I type these words, I have just received an email from a friend, also a mother, written in hurry and rage (you will note), with a weblink to an incredibly twee-looking new cookery book about mummies and daughters sharing recipes and laughter in an amazingly sunlit-dappled *cuisine* ... I will quote the email verbatim.

Sensitive readers should be warned, it may contain nuts:

> *DAISY for God's sake say you will write about this sort of SHIIIIIT in your mother book – look at it! Even the cover is so FUCKING SANCTIMONIOUS! AND I'm pretty sure her mother never made anything with fucking 'mascarpone' in it anyway, because GARLIC was barely even invented in the UK till the end of the bloody 70s!!!!!!!!!!!*

Mother love is ferocious, intense, fathomless, unconditional, absolute. It is no myth. *We know this!* But the pastel-shaded, guilt-driven, bake-your-own, bend-over-and-take-it-up-the-tailpipe saintliness that we have allowed to grow up around it is sheer humbug.

If it were in our interests to continue with the pretence, I would be more than happy to play along. But how can it be? Mothers are not saints. We never were.

## *Calling All Livestock*

I have said that that I am writing in defence of 'all the Mummies everywhere', and so I am. But Reading Parenting Books is about as middle class an activity as any on the planet. It's a veritable badge of membership, nothing less. And so, though I may be writing *in defence* of all the mummies everywhere, I'm writing with a likely reader in mind. And I'm going to piss off a fair few. The Mumgelicals, for example, who love nothing more than a (different kind of) parenting book; who believe in the myth of Perfect Motherhood, and in the righteous drama of their maternal selflessness – they may prefer to set this book aside. It is a parenting book. But it's not for them.

Above all, I suppose, it's for me, because I am tired of the guilty-dog simpering. And it's for my daughters, in the hope that when/if their turn comes, they won't feel, as some of my generation has, that they should stifle their human nature and their common sense – for the sake of repressive convention. And shucks – maybe (if you've read this far), it's for you too.

It's for all the women out there who, like me, feel torn: between their love for their child and a hunger for life, which appetite didn't simply extinguish because we became mothers. It's for the women who, like me, grew up taking their independence, equality, curiosity and individuality for granted, and who woke up one day, peed on a plastic stick, and discovered that all at once, the rules of engagement had changed. Intelligence, education, spirit and individuality were no longer required. By joining the sisterhood of Approved Mothers (whether we worked or didn't work) we were only really obliged to do two things: smile …

 And moo.

With their domineering stupidity and their inflexibly soppy demands, the Sentimentalists have held the stage for too long. I think it's time to add a dusting of reality (perhaps a sprinkling of garlic?) to the sickly-sweet debate.

I think it's time to burn those appalling maternity bras *if we feel so inclined*. And to kick back.

The Stepford Mummies can subjugate their education, curiosity, lust for life, equal claim to a small space in the universe … if that's what they want to do. They can swathe themselves in martyrdom and their offspring in Dettox-soaked bubble wrap – if they choose. Treat their children like flimsy little robo-gods, programmed not to question, not to create or to give back, but to *keep safe, and keep consuming*. If it's the only way they know how to live and love. So be it.

 But maybe the rest of us can do better than that. Because although we really, really, *really* love our kids ☺

… we are more than just their mothers.

## *What Are Children For?*

Depends who's asking, doesn't it? The CEO of Toys R Us, Sir

Jimmy Savile, you, me, Joseph Kony – or the Bishop of Rome.

Broadly speaking, I suppose, they're not for anything much, except for growing into adults. So that then they can have children of their own and, err, perpetuate the human race.

Which is nice.

But it doesn't really explain why, as individuals, we continue to go to the inconvenience of bringing our own children into the world. I can honestly say that 'perpetuating the human race' was not even at the bottom of my list of reasons for having children. It didn't feature at all.

Bearing in mind what an appalling impact children have on our finances, sex lives, friendships, ambitions, our bodies and our freedom – and bearing in mind the overwhelming sense of doom, the black cloud of world-at-an-endness that hovers between Western consciousness and the broken ozone layer – and bearing in mind that the planet is already horribly overpopulated, that Venice is sinking, the ice caps are melting, the welfare state is unaffordable, the politicians are crooks, the world economic contraction is a Braxton Hicks to what lies ahead, that retirement's a pipe dream, and we're all going to die of cancer in a hospital corridor, queuing for a superbug-infested bed ...

And bearing in mind that it's usually raining.

It seems extraordinary that we continue to breed at all.

And it begs the question: why? Why, above all, do Western women – with jobs and dreams, financial independence and reasonably full lives – *why do we put ourselves through it?*

21

Below is a list of possible motives. They are all I have been able to come up with so far.

- We are in love.

  The desire to give the love a physical form, and to create a life that forever unites us, can be hard to resist ... for the first baby at least. However, when said adored Unity arrives, even the most ardent lovers soon realise that such a romantic notion is really nothing more than that. The helpless, mewling, beloved product of our magical union isn't more or less than the sum of the two parts, but a separate entity all of its own.

  By the time any question of a second baby is being considered, the experience of bearing and caring for Baby Number 1 generally means that the high-falutin' superlove of early days has morphed – for better or worse – into something slightly different. Second babies tend to be born (and third and fourth) because by then – shucks – in for a penny, in for a pound. You have to pay the babysitter anyway, and Baby Number 1 could use the company. Added to which, of course, in years to come, Baby Number 1 may decide to emigrate to Australia.

- We like the idea of being surrounded by a loving family.

- We want to feel needed.

- We like taking care of helpless creatures.

- Everyone else is doing it. And it's a bit lonely being the only one without a baby.

- Other people's babies are cute and we want one of our own.

- Our job is boring and a new baby's a good excuse to resign.

- We qualify for maternity leave.

- We've reached a stage in life where something has to change – and it takes the pressure off coming up with something more imaginative.

- It seems like the right time and we might regret not having had a baby in years to come.

- Our partner wants a baby, and there'll be no peace until he gets it.

- Our partner wants a baby and we want to make him happy.

- Our partner wants a baby and threatens to find someone else to provide him with one, if we refuse.

- We're already pregnant and can't face having an abortion.

- We've already had an abortion and it will help us to feel better about that.

- A parent/close friend has just been told they are dying/has just died and it's brought on a Mortality Awareness Crisis. New life brings new hope.

- To trap a partner who might be thinking of abandoning us.

- To encourage someone to marry us ... (there may be an overlap with above).

- To take care of us in old age.

- It's a meal ticket!

- It guarantees a bigger divorce settlement (again, some overlap with above).

- We want to milk the welfare system for everything it's worth, and it seems like an effective way forward.

- As a source for organ-harvesting for a close family member.

- We're longing for an excuse to spend money and time in Mothercare.

- It satisfies a deep and primal desire to perpetuate if not the human race, then at least our own stake in it.

- Because life is meaningless and, at bottom, we are all painfully lonely. And children, with the hope and joy they bring, help to keep our absolute despair at bay.

Okay. Enough. I'm being excessively depressing. Perhaps.

No matter how you look at it, our reasons for bringing children into the world have nothing whatsoever to do with the interests of a yet-to-be-born baby, and everything to do with our own interests, or – which is the same thing – those of the people we happen to care about. Mothers have babies – despite environmentalist assertions that the world would be better if they didn't – because, for one reason or another, it suits us. (A pregnant Catholic who refuses abortion, by the way, or who rejects life-saving medication 'for the sake of' her unborn child, is acting according to her own adopted moral code, and out of fear for her own eternal soul. She is no more selfless than the rest of us. Just – dare I say it? A bit sillier.)

The point is, Mummies all, we are no less self-interested than the next man. So to speak.

And so what?

Well – nothing much. Except that it puts what can only be described as a spoke in the wheel of the Saintly Motherhood bandwagon, before said bandwagon's even pulled out of the station … And I find that rather liberating. We procreate, not for the benefit of our children, not for the pleasure of friends, not for the approval of health visitors, school teachers, or thin-lipped government advisers, but for myriad expediencies, all of which, as bandwagons to Rome, lead to the benefit, pleasure, comfort and approval – of ourselves.

Mother love, as discussed, is a beautiful thing, bringing with it an abundance of collateral goodness: patience, kindness, tenderness – and yes, self-sacrifice – but at the bottom of it all, we too are only human. And motherhood is all about us. So before we go any further – before we even start on the maternity bras – let's first toss our halos into the fire.

And discover how much lighter we feel without them.


## Martyr Mother Syndrome

Look at this mad thing.

It was quite fashionable for a while, among the Mumgelicals of America, to post the following message onto their Facebook page. It was a sort of 'Martyr Mom' mission statement, from what I can make out. Reminiscent of those bouncy stickers we used to Sellotape onto each other's backs in the playground, with 'Kick Me' written on them:

> *To all the UNSELFISH MOMS out there who traded sleep for dark circles, salon haircuts for ponytails, long showers for quick showers, late nights for early mornings, designer bags for diaper bags & WOULDN'T CHANGE A THING. Lets [sic] see how many Moms can actually post this. Moms who DON'T CARE about what they gave up and instead, LOVE what they got in return! Post this if you LOVE your LIFE as a mom.* ♥

Sick bags nicely disposed of? Local loony bins alerted?

Good.

Where do we begin?

It's absurd, clearly. And could be dismissed on grounds of a) illiteracy and b) breathtaking inanity. Nevertheless, in its clumsy way, it highlights what is a commonly held belief: that good motherhood requires, first and foremost, a denial of personal pleasure and a negation of the self.

What's especially offensive about this particular manifestation, however, aside from the hectoring tone and the gratuitous misogyny ('Let's see how many Moms can actually post this'), is the implication, often made, though rarely so inelegantly, that 'Unselfish Moms' should not simply rejoice in their children, but should rejoice in all they have given up to be mothers. As if the joy in the sacrifices (and what a drivelling list they present us with: *salon haircuts for ponytails, designer bags for diaper bags?*) were a prerequisite of bona fide motherly love, and that a mother who doesn't draw masochistic pleasure in such slavish self-denial, is not properly fulfilling her role.

Yes – we know it. Motherhood comes with a million small costs, requires a million different compromises and sometimes may even require taking a slightly shorter shower ... But there is something a little sinister about the way the kick-me brigade harps on. And it makes me wonder: why are they so aware of the costs in the first place? And, more to the point, *why oh why* must they insist on banging on about them so?

When I was just an awkward young gel, I went out with an awkward young lad whose parents owned a pub, which he often told me was struggling to stay afloat. One Saturday afternoon, he and I were watching telly, chewing through a shared beefburger that had been cooked for us in the pub's kitchen. 'If you were a customer eating this,' he suddenly announced, spraying ketchup and leather balls of mincemeat with each consonant, 'it would have cost you £6.95.'

I said, 'Really?' And then, quickly, 'Gosh, *thank you.*'

He said: 'No, no, *no.* I didn't mean for you to say *that.* I'm really, really happy you're eating it. That's what it's for! No! I was just saying ... This pub is probably about to go bust. Literally. Any minute. And that's quite a lot of money, isn't it? My parents could have sold this beefburger for £6.95.'

I thanked him again. (The pub never did go bust, by the way.) And felt most uncomfortable. Felt obliged to apologise for choosing the bloody thing, and then to praise its sawdust-quality deliciousness, and then, worst of all, to finish the bloody thing ... What, I wondered, was he hoping for in exchange for this unappetising piece of information?

In any other walk of life we laugh at them: the Pharisees, who make such a song and dance about the giving, and such a song and dance rejoicing at the cost ... We can't help but ask ourselves: *What are they really after*? What's in it for them?

And yet somehow, the Martyr Mothers get away with it. Partly, I suppose, because for the fathers, at least, what price a little sanctimony, if it means escaping from their share of the parenting chores? And partly because the other mothers – who take on their motherly chores in a more brusque and businesslike fashion, and are often in search of short cuts – tend to feel a little sheepish about their anti-zeitgeist SELFISH MOM status. I know I do. Or did. It's what drove me to write this book.

When the prevailing culture encourages mothers to confuse love for subjugation, and endlessly reinforces the message that a mother who puts her own needs first – *under any circumstances* – is a bad mother and a freak of biological nature, we know in our heads and hearts that it can't make sense, because we never actually stopped being humans. Despite this, it's tempting to nod agreeably and say nothing, to smile obediently and shuffle quietly on ...

Take, for example:

## Me Time

It's a ludicrous phrase – and these days, to be fair, it's used as often in jest as in earnest. Nevertheless, the notion remains. And it reeks of a very particular deodorised-panty-pad, simpering-style femininity. Men don't talk about having 'Me Time'. Why, their entire lives are made up of 'Me Time'! Ha. Ha.

Me Time is the speciality, above all, of Busy Mums; mums who spend all day rushing around worrying, and who, every now and then, it is generally agreed, deserve a little break from doing things for others: a few quiet minutes, after dropping the kids at school, to sit down with a cup of coffee and a muffin, perhaps, and the new edition of *Grazia* magazine. Or, better yet, an afternoon in a health spa with the girls, discussing hubby and kids to the soft sounds of electronic lounge music.

And hell – I'm not saying there's anything wrong with any of that. Each to her own. I am only saying that implicit in the Me Time notion, no matter what form it takes, is the assumption that all *non* 'Me Time' is Other People's Time.

But of course it isn't.

Yes, mothers spend much of their time tending to the requirements of their family. (Martyr mothers, far more time than they need to.) But then again, most *adults* spend much of their time tending to the requirements of others. It's called 'Being an Adult'. It's called 'Having a Job'. Mothers care for their children, not because of some nature-given selflessness exclusive to them, but if anything, because of the opposite. It's in a mother's interests to tend to her children because she cares *massively* – more than anyone else – about her children's welfare.

It's basic self-interest for a mother to take care of her children. We look after what we care for. *Me Time* is all the time. It's called 'My Life', and it is always up to us how we decide to spend it.


## Happy Mum Means Happy Kids! ☺

Indeed it often does. But – lest we forget – it's not the *only* reason Mum might attempt to be happy ☺. Mum might, for example, attempt to be happy because, like other 'people' who 'aren't Mums', she is also 'a human being' ☹.


## Guilt

Several years ago, a nasty dose of maternal guilt drove me, briefly, to join the Stay-at-Home league of mothers. I got rid of the childcare, we moved to the country and for a year I did almost no paid work at all.

I baked cakes.

Attended coffee mornings.

Cooked wholesome dinners for my children.

Examined the local wildlife.

Counted sheep.

And watched an amazing amount of telly.

It wasn't simply the change in my finances that was difficult. In fact, for much of that time, I was still being paid for work I had completed before my somewhat premature retirement. As any newly unemployed person would tell you, it was the loss, too, of all the things I had previously taken for granted: independence, intellectual stimulation, a sense of personal achievement, personal identity and individual status ... Also, the unwelcome emergence of a sudden, horrifying reliance on the other half, not yet for money (though that would come), but for news and contact with the rest of the world. We had started out, he and I, before all this maternal angst had led us to the green fields, as equals and friends in the great adventure of life. In a matter of months, I had transformed into a cartoon cliché of the Discontented Housewife.

We lived in a lovely house (Perfect For The Kids) in a well-to-do corner of this green and pleasant land, within an hour or so of London. It was high-priced commuter land. And so, during the week, while the menfolk went off to work, I lived, as full-time mothers tend to, in a world peopled only by women, every one of us on the same small treadmill. We talked about the kids ... and worried about the kids ... and talked about the kids ... and talked about what was best for the kids ... and talked about what was not best for the kids. At a stroke, my universe had shrunk to include nothing but the school and the house, and the house and the school. Everything beyond that had simply disappeared.

I began to resent my husband's access to the wider world, felt jealous of his business trips away, and quite soon, aware of how little I had to say to the still-toiling girlfriends I had left behind, lost the confidence to make contact with them. It was the loneliest – and actually the most boring – year of my life. I had tried in earnest to be the sort of mother I thought I was meant to be, fulfilled by the delights and blessings of motherhood, and of motherhood alone, but I came up against a major obstacle. Me.

Plenty of women offered counsel and comfort, and plenty understood. *'Oh God, it's hell,'* they agreed. 'But you get used it! It takes about five years.' (Weirdly, a time period they all seemed independently to agree upon.) ... 'The first five years are really tough. But after that *you get used to it*. These days,' they said, *'I honestly wouldn't have it any other way ...'*

*FIVE years?!* I thought. *But I could be dead in three!*

I was lucky. Being self-employed, I had a clear route out of the situation. Added to which, for some reason, I've never been particularly embarrassed about saying, 'I fucked up.' Which I clearly had. I didn't want to spend five years nestling into a self-imposed lobotomy.

Several years later, a well-known radio presenter, a doyenne of feminism, or so I had always assumed, asked me during a live broadcast if I felt 'guilty' about dragging the family back to London after our failed adventure; and I am still infuriated by the question. 'A family can only be as happy as its least-happy member,' I told her. But I wish I had said more. Or less, actually. The point is – I was miserable. *That's* the point, and it should be enough. Would she have asked my husband if he felt guilty? Would she have asked my children, if they were the ones who had been suffering? I suspect not. Mothers are expected to put up with their personal wretchedness, so long as the rest of the family is happy. And that is not feminism. That is cruel and archaic nonsense.

It happens I know of another family who made a similar move from London to the country around the same time; the man commuted, the woman became a housewife and was miserable. When she confided her unhappiness, her husband said: 'But this move isn't about *you*. It's about the kids.' She was foolish enough to believe him, and though she wears a brave face, it is painfully obvious to see that she is still miserable today. It's too bad. Or not. It fills me with rage, actually. But there you have it. It's the choice she made.

Anyway, we moved back to London: rather poorer than we had left it, what with all the buying and selling of houses. The children returned to their old school. I returned to my writing desk. And here we still are today.

## ... And *More* Guilt (To Work Or Not To Work?)

Fathers don't feel it. Why do we? Somewhere along the line modern mothers have accepted guilt as an inevitable part of the parenting package, as if guilt were the price we have to pay for equality and choice. But it makes not a jot of sense. We give life; we feed, clothe, comfort and protect, we care for our children the best we can; we lavish on them our unconditional, absolute, everlasting love. And yet, we feel it is not enough, because in this neurotic uber-parenting culture *nothing will ever be enough* – nothing short of a sort of maternal suttee.

It means we tend to feel a little divided, and are perhaps not as straightforward as we could be, when it comes to the thorny matter of careers – or paid work.

My family – husband, three children and I – leads a comfortable, middle-class life. The money I earn probably makes up a third of our household income and without it, much in our household, including the house itself, would have to change. But do I *have* to work, or is it a choice?

Working mothers tend to begin all discussions on this tricky subject from the defensive premise that they don't have any choice in the matter.

And listen – here I am, earning money at a job which perhaps a lot of people might love to do. It's not to say I haven't had a bunch a stultifyingly boring and unpleasant jobs in the past – I have. But not for many years. And in any case, clearly, I am sitting kind of pretty today. I know it. Which means that what I am about to say lies on a par, I imagine, on the *Really Fucking Irritating* graph, with Conservative government ministers telling impoverished single mothers not to go food shopping when they're hungry. Nevertheless, I've got to say it, because our attitudes to work are so entwined with our maternal guilt and martyrdom … And the fact is we *do* have a choice.

No stay-at-home mother in this country is ever going to starve, and nor will her children. Here in Britain we have free education, we have the NHS and we have a welfare state, specifically to prevent such a thing from happening. Once her children are of school age, a mother may be chivvied and bullied to a handful of unwanted job interviews, but she can botch them if she wants to. On Income Support, she and her children will certainly live in poverty. But they would not be destitute. It would never be a matter of life and death. Which means (unwedge the panties! It's simply a statement of fact!) all working mothers – single, unsupported mothers without a bean to their name, as well as mothers currently hitched to A.N. Earning-Other as well as lucky cows like me – go to work, not, *to cover the cost of living*, but to cover the cost of living *better*. In other words, we work because we prefer it to the alternative. We work because we want to.

I only wish we could take a leaf out of the L'Oréal ad and apply its perky reasoning, not simply to the buying of beauty products, but to the embracing of life itself.

Say it loud: I work because I want to work, because I prefer it to the alternative; I work for autonomy, independence, self-respect, in some cases for personal enjoyment, and above all, for CASH. I go to work and earn a living because it's preferable to staying at home, and in the long run, more gratifying. I work ... *because I'm worth it!* Dammit.

We working mothers make quite a hullabaloo about how exhausting it is to be us – all that juggling and distressing of cakes at midnight. (And I shall be returning to the midnight cake-distressing later.) Well, even if it is exhausting (which it is), it doesn't have to be half as exhausting as we make it – err, see title of book. Added to which, if you ask me – if you ask most of us, in private, post a few glasses of Truth Serum, and assuming it hasn't been a spectacularly bad day at work – almost any level of exhaustion-while-juggling is preferable to the powerless and confined stay-at-home alternative. Pretty much anything is probably better, as most men would agree, than a life of unpaid domestic drudgery and dependency, in a world which rarely extends beyond the kitchen and the school gate.

So I sent out a Tweet (nothing like doing a bit of research, eh?), asking the mothers out there to share with me their thoughts: did they work and wish they didn't, or vice versa? Were they happy with the choices they had made?

Nothing very surprising came back, except for this breathtakingly patronising message from a middle-aged man, whose opinion I hadn't sought in the first place:

*'Daisy, trust me. Women who work. Don't want to.'*

But never mind him. Other than that ... there were bits and bobs of frothing self-righteousness from the evangelical stay-at-home brigade – the same women, I can only imagine (and there were many), who a hundred years ago might have joined the Women's Anti-Suffrage League – and a clutch of replies from the middle ground, all confirming what anyone with half a brain would expect. Replies from non-workers were more plentiful, more wistful – and less certain. Replies from workers were more succinct – and sounded more confident.

But almost all of them dwelled on maternal guilt:

'I work p-t, have 3 kids (6,5,3). Feel guilty about being happy to go to work after 5yrs at home'

'I've worked full time, part time and stayed at home. Staying at home def the hardest, but felt guilty with all of them'

'Non-working mum. Feel guilty about unfulfilled ambition/ guilt for no plan now kids getting older. What next?'

What next indeed? The guilt is everywhere, insidious and self-defeating. It is getting us nowhere. It's a ridiculous and unhappy situation. And obviously – or it seems obvious to me – we should fight it. Shouldn't we? ... At least, we should identify guilt as the enemy and attempt to turn our backs on the self-hate fest: stop beating ourselves up about where we fail as mothers and celebrate where we succeed. Or better yet – stop measuring our performance altogether and just *get on with it*, confident that the ordinary, irrepressible love we feel for our children will help us to muddle through. And along the way, I think we should make no bones about trying (at least) to reclaim whatever we might of ourselves – not simply as mothers, but as adults, equals and individuals in a shared universe.

It's a particular form of torture, leaving our babies and toddlers behind. No matter where it is, or with whom – a grandmother, a nanny, a daycare centre – their cries as we abandon them sound the same.

And they're horrible. Visceral. Like someone pouring vinegar into the veins. Walking away from them is far harder than resisting a plate of hot, buttery crumpets when you're hungry.

Self-denial – with guilt on top – is no laughing matter. But there are dividends. And *as we all know*, those heartbreaking cries pass very quickly.

'She'll be fine in a minute,' the carer says, clutching our bawling baby, silently longing for us to bugger off and stop protracting the wretched scene. 'Don't you worry. She'll be laughing in a second!'

And of course we know it's true. In a daycare centre, there'll be other babies to goggle at and innumerable bits of brightly coloured plastic to amuse. At home, with an au pair, our child will have something else to distract her. The telly, most likely. Followed, no doubt, by that perennial low-cost toddler diversion: the feeding of the ducks ...

The point is, either way, within a couple of minutes or rather less, those heart-shattering, blood-curdling cries will have turned to gentle hiccups, and until we cross their eyeline again, our beloved babies will have more or less forgotten we ever existed.

It's wonderful to feel needed: one of the great pulls and pleasures of motherhood. But let's not get above ourselves. Feeding of the Ducks is the Feeding of the Ducks. No matter who's holding out the bag of stale bread ...

I have just this morning read an irritating article in one of the broadsheets, written by an older, female journalist, which appears to be suggesting that there are really two sorts of women, or maybe, even, three different genders. There are women; *clever and effective* women; and men. Clever and effective women, or 'Alpha' women (as she calls them) 'perhaps less softened by oestrogen', don't mind being away from their children. Whereas 'other women – *most* women ... passionately feel a maternal need to be at home with their children, to hear their children's first words, to be there for supper with their teenagers every day'. Hankies out please, ladies. Beta ladies, that is. Time for a Beta-blub.

Simultaneously patronising, sentimental, idiotic and cruel, it's just another sample, from another weekend's newspapers, of the background chunter against which all mothers – working, non-working – Alpha to Omega – have to try to find our peace.

I refrained from emailing her my thoughts (because, note here, writing angry messages to people you don't know is a tragic way to pass the time). But I was sorely tempted. I wanted to ask her, *Why. Why would you write this? You are a mother. You KNOW how painful it is for a mother to imagine she is in some way less natural or less loving than other mothers; that she might, in some way be letting her own children down. YOU KNOW ABOUT THE GUILT. So why do you write this sexist, sentimental bullshit? Why do you want to make other women feel abnormal for being people as well as mothers? Why do you want them to feel that they have failed?*

Added to which, of course (as any first year history student could tell you), the idea that a woman should want to fill her days watching over her own children so very intensively, to sob and hyper-ventilate over their every munch and gurgle, is really very new; a faintly degenerate invention to fill the domestic void created by washing machines. Until my own mother's generation, upper- and middle-class women (anyone, frankly, who could afford it) employed nannies and nursery maids to do most of the grunt work for them – the same work that modern mothers are supposed to find so fulfilling. Working-class women, overloaded by grunt work already, had more pressing demands on their time, along with an extended family, and (pre the community-wrecking tower blocks) neighbours long known to one another to help keep an open eye.

Modern mothers walk a tightrope of tact. Aware of how inadequate we all feel, both worker bees and the stay-at-home variety, we tend to keep our own counsel on the delicate matter of which is preferable: to work or not to work. Everyone is different, we say. 'Female empowerment' is all about, well – not being horrid to each other, applauding one another no matter what, never really saying anything controversial ... and then bitching about each other's choices behind each other's backs.

To work or not to work? Well now, I may be wrong (I suppose) ... But, if you took the maternal guilt completely out of the equation; if you knew your children were in good hands; if you could work, but with balance, not excessively, and cover your childcare costs with something left over; and assuming the work wasn't actively unpleasant, then *for so many of us* (YES, I KNOW, not for all), it's got to be a no-brainer. Self-sufficiency and independence and a connection with the wider world breed confidence and self-respect, which breeds good cheer.

*''Tis ever common,'* (as Shakespeare so cleverly pointed out) *that men are merriest when they are from home.'*

*'Tis ever* – something working mothers have been slowly, quietly discovering for themselves for some time now.

*'Tis ever* – a secret, which our maternal guilt, encouraged by the spiteful, stupid commentaries of journalists like the one above, has prevented us from sharing with our homebound sisters all this time.

*'Tis ever* – something the men have known all along, of course.

And since Recent Studies can say whatever you want them to say, and there really appears to be no conclusive evidence to suggest that the children of full-time mothers fare any better than their more neglected, but equally adored playmates, you have to ask yourself this: when life is so short, and the world is so wide, and confidence and independence and EARNING MONEY feel so good – what's to stay at home *for*?

Added to which (I'll come clean) ...

The more working mothers there are, the fewer non-working mothers there will be, which means fewer well-intentioned but inessential Mummy Tasks concocted by them to fill the days, which we worker bees then have to run around desperately trying to find time to do ... or desperately apologise for failing to do ... It means fewer letters in satchels asking for home-baked cakes for the cake stand or home-made play dough for the nursery, fewer requests for nicely decorated jam jars for the bazaar, amusing home-made Easter bonnets for the Easter bonnet parade, theme-coloured bear outfits for the Canadian

Bear Awareness Week project – and no more three-line whips to attend midweek, early afternoon singing/swimming/dancing shows ... Unnecessary parental input will, by necessity, be pared to a sensible minimum.

And the children themselves will be left in peace, in their carefree, childish paradise, to make the hats, bake the fucking cakes, and do their frigging homework for themselves.

It's a win-win.


## The Unspoken Battle

It's called the 'Mummy Wars' in the media, which is patronising but not inaccurate. It's the delicate – and unwinnable – battle between the mothers who work and the mothers who don't. Mostly, we keep a fragile truce. We try our best to get along. But beneath the smiles and grimaces, the apologies and the 'Not-to-Worry!'s, there is a small cauldron of mutual distrust and resentment bubbling away ... No doubt my reference to Inessential Mummy Tasks above didn't much help to ease the peace between the two camps, either. It was provocative of me. Clearly.

But then again ...

The difficulty, of course, is that by the mere fact of their existence, each group undermines the strivings of the other. If a woman can be a good mother and also hold down a job, then what the hell are the full-time mothers *doing* with themselves all day? On the other hand, if there really *is* enough mothering to fill an entire existence, could it mean the children of working mothers are missing out?

I was discussing this book – and the incredibly fragile truce that exists between the earning and non-earning factions – with two other mothers, both of whom were clever, reasonable, decent women (under normal circumstances). Both had young children and full-time jobs.

The conversation started well enough:

'Oh dear yes, it is a minefield isn't it ...' [or something along these lines]

'You feel you're being rude when you're not available to help out with things ...

– so you're endlessly having to apologise ...

– and endlessly having to say thank you ...

– and then *they* say "not to worry" and of course they're only being helpful.

But you want to say, "Well, but I wouldn't have to worry, if only you'd stop creating so many pointless little tasks for me to do."'

Hahaha ...

At which point the conversation took a turn.

'Sometimes, on my way to work,' one of us declared, 'I walk past the mothers in their gym kits, sitting round having coffee with each other, and I want to pick up their frigging cappuccinos and pour them on their heads.

'I sometimes fantasise about hooking them up onto some kind of electrical circuit and whacking up the voltage, so their hair actually stands on end. It might wipe the smug look off their faces just for a second.'

43

Okay – it was just a moment! A nasty little moment at the end of a long week. Born of insecurity, no doubt, and irritability and jealousy and pack behaviour, and – fuck it, let's call it 'juggle-fatigue'. Plus it was quite funny. I have no doubt that, from time to time, the other side feels no less ferocious about us, as they stand under a tent in the playground in pouring rain, manning the National Reading Week Tuesday Lunchtime second-hand book exchange stall ... once again ... I'm sure they would dearly love to take our self-important BlackBerrys and shove them – too bad.

I happen to be writing this a couple of days after Cherie Blair climbed up on her hind legs and made what I assume, from the media's spit and hiss, to have been a remarkably tactless speech about the superiority of working mothers over what she fatuously refers to as 'yummy mummies'. *Daily Mail Online* called it an 'astonishing attack'.

So I have just Googled the speech. And what she actually said was:

> 'Every woman needs to be self-sufficient ... you hear these yummy mummies talk about being the best possible mother and they put all their effort into their children. I also want to be the best possible mother, but I know that my job as a mother includes bringing my children up so actually they can live without me.'

Which, actually, isn't that incendiary is it? Not half as incendiary as the headlines that surrounded it. I'm not even quite sure what she's saying – or even if she's saying anything at all. 'Cherie Blair attacks "yummy mummies"', it said in the *Telegraph*.

In any case, not even slightly surprisingly, all hell has broken out. Women on both sides of the Crazy Fence are frothing with rage. Cherie's words have led to a counter-attack from the 'On Behalf of the Stay-at-Home Mummy' brigade. I notice in one of the broadsheets, a drippy-looking New Dad has presumed to join the fray, desperately sucking up to his stay-at-home girlfriend, we have to assume, by noting, breathlessly, how silly and conceited successful working mothers tend to be, and how jolly saintly and difficult it is to be a Stay-at-Home-Mum.

Silly sod.

He can fuck off, clearly.

As indeed can the ridiculous Cherie. Or not. Between you and me, I rather love her.

But anyway –

All in all, I think, on this important matter the fundamental survival rule can be summed up in one, sweet, single sound: *shhhhhhhhhhh.*

Least said, soonest mended. We mother as we see fit. *AND WE ALL LOVE OUR CHILDREN*. That's what we need to hold on to.

The good news is, at least, beneath the rage and the bluster, we all definitely know we're right.

## *Yeah. But No. But Can I Also Just Say ...*

What happens to a full-time mother when her children finally leave home? Perhaps her spouse, assuming there is one, retires from his job at the same time? And perhaps, despite her long-standing withdrawal from a world beyond her children's school gates, she still has plenty to say that's worth listening to; and the two still have some things in common, other than the love of their fully grown children? And perhaps they have money to spare (though how, I don't quite know, with only one half of the household bringing it in) and perhaps Hubby and Mum buy a round-trip ticket to see the world together. How lovely! But that can't last for ever.

And then what? She's still young: in her fifties, probably. That's a lot of years left to live without having anything much to do. Except wait ... for children busy leading their own lives to feel sufficiently guilty or broke – or homesick – to want to come back for a visit.

Sometimes, I look at our family-sized house and imagine it empty, as it will be when the children have all flown the nest ... And I am filled with misery. Nothing could ever fill the void – all the life and hope and merriment they bring to the place. But at least, as long as I am working, there will be something to keep me occupied when they have left, and – better yet – a reason for me to stay engaged with the world.

*'Everyone I know goes away in the end'*, sang Johnny Cash, on one of his more cheerful jags. He had a point ... At any rate, our

darling children are certainly *supposed* to go away eventually.

Better to make like a Boy Scout. Have a life. Be Prepared.

Get a job?

## *Childcare*

My name is D—, I am the mother of three, and for a long time, at least until a few months ago, I employed full-time help with house and children. Financially, it was a killer, but – at the time – it made sense. Now the children are older, they can help to look after each other and we muddle through. Really, *muddle*. It's fine. Except in the holidays.

Over the years, depending on the ages of the children and what money was coming in, I have experimented with most of the childcare options available: daycare drop-in, nanny share, live-out au pair, live-in au pair, take-it-in-turns-with-another parent share ... A mix-'n'-match of all of the above. And in the green fields of commuter land, for one year only, no childcare at all. Whatever worked – or worked well enough – simply had to do ... No arrangement was perfect. But then again, nor was I.

People sometimes politely asked, as they do all working mothers, 'Goodness-gracious-but-how-do-you-manage?' (I don't know how she does it!) When I told them, 'Well, I have a *lot* of help,' (duh) they often look rather surprised. Sometimes even a little embarrassed ... But how the hell else would I get any work done? Every mother of young children who works has to use help, for which, at some point – unless she happens to be among the fortunate few, blessed with a saintly relation willing to step in absolutely free – money, or payment in kind, must change hands.

And yet, somehow, the obvious truth of this – working mothers' fundamental dependence on outsourcing their childcare – remains a faintly dirty secret; something that is skirted around in public, even by the working mothers themselves, and is regarded with a faint mix of disdain, mockery and/or envy by almost everyone else.

It doesn't much matter what the men think. Or not about this. But it matters what we think of ourselves. It's impossible to work and look after children simultaneously. Therefore, unless we believe mothers should withdraw from the world and return to their kitchens again, we need to employ help.

I think it's mean, and a little cowardly, when high-profile women refuse to lead the way on this, come clean and admit to all the help they have. And of all the high-profile women who would like us to believe they raise their children in a cloud of gravity-defying magic dust, I think Michelle Obama may be the most infuriating culprit.

Her children are older now, but since the beginning she has always told us that she doesn't employ a nanny – because the First Family Grandma moved into the White House along with the First Family. Well. Bully for Grandma, eh?

Except I don't suppose the First Grandma sews on the games kit name tags, does she? Or checks that the right uniform is ready and ironed for school the following morning; or goes to the drugstore to stock up on lice eradicator? Time-consuming childcare duties each and every one. And if Granny's not doing it, and Michelle's not doing it, and we must all hope Barack has something more pressing to do with his time, then who do you suppose is? Call him/her what you will: a Harvard Business School 'civil servant', or a good ol'-fashioned nursery maid ... Who cares? She surely isn't called Mom. Does the fact that somebody else in the Obama household stocks up on Elastoplast and Calpol make Michelle a less loving mother? Hardly. But the fact that she's not straightforward about what it takes for her to play a part in the wider world, that she won't speak up about working mothers' dependence on childcare, makes her a less than perfect feminist, without a doubt.

## Childcare, Cost Of

Feels astronomical when you're shelling out for it. Then again, why wouldn't it? Looking after children, as we know, is more gruelling than most work. In a reasonably fair society (when you take the bankers out of the equation), paying someone else's wage out of your own, post tax, is likely to be pretty painful. So it goes. There are a hundred different ways to approach the problem, none of which is ideal; some of which are fractionally less exorbitant than others. (And now you know, eh? Nobody calls *me* unhelpful.) I have only two points to raise, or rather, questions to pose, on this indelibly depressing subject.

1) Did you know (of course you did, everybody does) that

a man can claim the cost of his chauffeur against tax, but a woman cannot claim the cost of a nanny or other childcare?

2) When a woman becomes a mother, and she and her partner consider the viability of her returning to work, why is it usually assumed that the childcare costs of the new baby – wot, without wishing to state the obvious, it took two parents to conceive – should be covered and/or justified by the income of the mother alone? Why is that?

Moving on.

The irritations and expenses of childcare become less consuming (until the school holidays), by the time we find ourselves experiencing the myriad pleasures of life at the ...

## *School Gate*

We are treated to a constant stream of articles, studies, movies, vacuous chick-lit novels and amusing comedy TV shows about the appalling pressures heaped on 'normal' mothers at school gates across the land. 'Normal' mothers, it seems, have a rotten time of it out there! In fact (a recent study revealed ...) an ASTONISHING thirty-nine per cent of all mothers are made to feel like 'complete failures' by the other mothers at the school gate ...

It seems hard to believe. Also, it makes me wonder: whoever framed such an odious question? And *why*? Has any of us ever been asked if we felt like 'utter failures' at any other of life's relatively ordinary pit stops? At the doctor's surgery, in the office canteen, at the bus stop, in the gym? I certainly haven't.

But I've often been asked about the 'hell' of the school gate. Why is that?

Two words sisters: endemic misogyny. Oh yeah.

Come the start of each new academic year, women journalists who really ought to know better are wheeled out to whip up the annual other-mother hate fest, and to discuss, in earnest voices, the difficulties of surviving 'drop off' intact. 'Other Mothers' (i.e., All Mothers, Except for Nice, Reasonable Little Me) are presented to us as caricatures of idiocy, snobbery, cut-throat competitiveness and petty-minded malice; monster women, who judge and condemn one another on the strength of their school run hair-dos and ability to remember packed lunches ...

But honestly, who *are* all these ridiculous women? I don't recognise them. And if they really do exist (I've never spotted them, outside any of the seven schools and nursery schools that my children have between them attended), then why, when they're patently absurd, do other women – the nice little reasonable ones – give them the time of day? Why would we give a damn what they think?

The problem stems, I suppose, from the usual sense of maternal inadequacy and guilt that bubbles beneath the simpering, smiling surface in us all. Our sense of loserly-ness (new word) has to find an outlet somewhere; so maybe we turn on each other and maybe, in the short term, it alleviates our sense of inadequacy. But in the long run, without wishing to state the obvious, it can only feed the loserly fire.

After all, if a mother turns up with an organic snack prepared each morning, with her trousers on the right way round, and some smart mascara on, does it mean she's doing a better job at raising her children than we are? Does it mean she's a better mother, or a better woman? Does it mean she has superior children? These questions are simply too goofy to merit answers. She's just another person, clever at early morning trousers, managing things her way, and trying very hard to raise the sort of child she wants to raise according to the rules and standards that she considers important.

The other day, a friend of mine accidentally bounced a cheque on one of her class mothers, who was collecting money (astronomical amounts) for a parents' evening-out shindy. It's easily done. I have done it often. But the mother doing the collecting had not, presumably. Gleefully appalled, she cc'd the entire class list when she emailed my friend to tell her the news:

> 'I have just received from the bank the cheque for £60 you gave me with the instruction "payment stopped" on it. I am not sure of the reason for this. However, it would be appreciated if you could please give £60 in cash to myself asap, as the invoices need to be paid.'

*What a bitch, eh?*

I have to assume that my friend, who can sometimes be abrasive, had unwittingly offended her at some previous juncture. My friend isn't bothered by what the school gate thinks of her financial management skills nor the depth of her pocket but at the same time, the malice of said mother cc'ing the entire class depressed her, and it depresses me too.

There is malice wherever humans fester. Significantly less – in my experience – at a school gate, than in a newspaper office. The temptation to turn the above incident into a misogynist other-mother bitch-fest is hard to resist ... but to what end?

We don't have to be friends with the mothers at the school gate. In fact, in this new, technological age, we barely need to talk to one another at all.

If our adorable little children happen to want to spend time in each other's houses, for example, a simple exchange of amiable texts between mothers and/or carers can get us through:

'Hi there! Is Frou Frou [fill in name as appropriate] free for tea at ours on Thurs?'

'Yes she is. Thank you so much. Shall I pick her up around six?'

I simply *cannot see* what could be frightening about that.

Also, by the way (and actually this is what infuriates me most), while we women insist on airing our misogynist insecurities so publicly, alternately whingeing and going for each other's throats, what are the men doing beneath their auto-soothing, not-really-listening, not-to-worry-babe mumblings? Rubbing their hands together in glee. Of course. It's win-win for them. Divide and Rule ... It was ever thus.

Thirty-nine per cent of *all mothers* are made to feel like 'complete failures' by the other mothers at the school gate?

Really? It's a *school gate* for crying out loud! Peopled by fellow mothers, some brighter and some kinder than others, but each one ferreting for air beneath her own invisible shroud of guilt and uncertainty, each one only present because *she really, really loves her kids* ☺ ...

Mega-Nice? Mega-Evil? Or maybe just something mega-inbetween?

How tough can it really be?

## Supermothers (And The SuperSupers)

Having said all that ... some mothers are mega nightmares. And some generalisations are unavoidable. More or less.

And I can't write an ENTIRE BOOK on the subject of modern mothering without taking a few pot shots at the Supers. Rather I could – and I *would* (honest) except every woman I have spoken to about this book has asked me to have a crack at them, and after all these years, biting my tongue and grimacing politely in the face of their awful, awful, *awfulness* ...

I can't resist.

Not all Supers are equally awful. Some are more awful than others. And although they make more noise than everyone else put together (it's why we can't help but notice them), in the great wash of mothers-at-school-gates, they form only a tiny group.

In my mind I have a prototype – an amalgamation-concentrate of all the rich, bossy, loud and pointlessly over-organised mothers I've ever encountered. And they're not monsters. *I suppose*. They just happen to share some monstrous qualities that seriously piss other people off.

Like so much in our culture, good and bad, the original Supers – for the sake of clarity, let's call them the 'SuperSupers' – hark from across the Herring Pond. In the past ten or fifteen years, they've come over in droves, with their banker husbands, and there are thousands here in the capital today, leading the way. London's private schools are teeming with them.

The British adaptation, meanwhile, is catching up fast. In some ways, actually, they are even more awful. The main difference being – at any rate, this is what I suspect – that they get out of bed just a tiny tad later than their American sisters. Because, although equally 'super' in other respects, they don't seem to bother with the same levels of personal grooming. The implication being (I have always assumed) that for the SuperBritMums, self-adornment is simply too trivial a task when compared to the vast and vital other responsibilities they face each morning: getting the kids to school earlier than everyone else, bellies groaning with appropriately healthful breakfasts. I find the British Supermothers, with their graceless, English, barking voices, even more depressing than the American version. Puffy and grey-faced, and perma-disapproving, they look like the battleaxes they really are. No Botox or fillers for them! Christ no! Nothing so frivolous! Just a few token lady accessories, chucked onto their bossy frames: valuable earrings, fussy overcoats, ridiculous leather boots, always noticeably expensive, always mysteriously irrelevant and unflattering.

It so happens (it might explain any excessive harshness in the above) that I'm still feeling a bit bashed around post-reprimand, last weekend, from one of their ilk, having inadvertently collided with one of her intricately laid plans regarding party bags.

'You didn't RSVP in time. That's the problem,' she said, when I arrived to pick up my daughter from the party. There was a two-themed choice of after-party 'party bag', she explained, bossiness and rage radiating off her like a desert heat. A *Star Wars* after-party farty-bag – and – er, a different one.

I said, 'Gosh, I'm so sorry.'

She said, 'If you'd RSVP'd in time we could've given her the party bag she wants.'

I said, 'Well she'll be delighted with either ... theme ... of party bag I'm sure.'

She said, 'Well, she wanted a *Star Wars,* but at this stage I can't be certain we have a *Star Wars* to spare.'

There followed a five-minute monologue, detailing which guest had RSVP'd within the correct timeframe, requesting what party bag and why. I had apologised three times, before she agreed to relinquish any party bag at all and we were finally free to leave.

The party bag, by the way, is still lying, only half-emptied and long forgotten, in a pile of sweet wrappers in the back of the car.

If I may return to the prototype?

Supermothers arrive ahead of the gaggle for the morning 'drop off' (as they importantly refer to it), sometimes wearing shiny running kit, always looking on top of things. They talk loudly and often incessantly, either to each other, organising 'play dates' with the urgency of world leaders discussing their withdrawal from Afghanistan, or to their children, issuing instructions, in tense, perky, ultra-reasonable voices. And every morning, it seems, they have something new, earnest and vital to impart to the children's form teacher, so they stand at the entrance to the classroom, necks out like turkeys, blocking the doorway and stopping anybody else from getting in or out.

They book the best slots at the parents' evenings, usually before anyone else even knows there's a parents' evening planned. They send out 'save the date' emails in advance of their children's birthday party invitations. And, if they're not abroad during school holidays (which thankfully they generally are), they send round-robins to the 'mums' with fun suggestions, often requiring children to be driven to unnecessary places at inconvenient times of the day, to do pointless activities that almost certainly cost money.

They organise expensive skill-enhancing activities for their children every weekday after school except – and we really ought to know it, because they've told us a hundred times – the third Tuesday of every month. And for those third Tuesdays, they organise 'Tuesday play dates' weeks, sometimes months, in advance. They do their children's homework for them, especially – or most noticeably – if the homework is craft-related. And they strut into school with their ludicrous 3D-papier-mâché models of Mount Vesuvius like they think they're fucking Damien Hirst ...

Deep breath.

Trouble is, in the egocentric whirlwind of efficiency that surrounds them, they may not know it, or even much care, but they make some, if not most, or even all of us feel like total losers.

Every mother I know has a Supermother horror story. Every mother to whom I mentioned this book has wanted to share with me a case study ... and it would be fun to pause – just for a moment – to wallow in this festival of sister-hating viciousness.

But we mustn't.

Or maybe just a mini-wallow. So I can tell you about the Super who organises thrice-weekly after-school maths classes for her six-year-old son ... And about the cluster of Supers at a smart London prep school (Must Not Name It), who took umbrage at the itchiness of the emblem-embroidered regulation woollen sweaters and campaigned *successfully* to have the same sweaters issued in cashmere ... Or about the rich Super who, having elbowed her son into the best state school in the area, then turned her attention to the European Courts to facilitate his right not to pay for his own school uniform ... Or about the woman who has an Excel spreadsheet, charting her child's food intake and measuring it against the hours he sleeps that night ...

The fundamental belief of Supermotherdom, it seems, is that the world can and must be moulded to facilitate their own child's path through life. And what's so *irritating* is that these women appear to possess limitless supplies of all the necessary resources – time, money and brute-faced shamelessness – to ensure that they bring it about.

Supers aren't stupid. Or not in the conventional sense. Often, they are highly educated. Often, pre-children, they had impressive, high-earning careers of their own. Now, that same efficiency and drive is being focused on creating perfect children. And with all the money and energy, all the care, self-discipline and detailed attention these women pour into the task, it's hardly surprising that they succeed. Supermummies create a Superbreed: a Supermummy Superprogeny ... a bit whiny and joyless, I would opine; but nonetheless good at an awful lot of things. Good at everything, actually, which requires private tuition, and concentrated, dedicated adult intercession. Other children, with lazier, busier and/or more impoverished mothers cannot hope to compete.

... So it is that the self-perpetuation of the Supers continues. They win places to the best schools, and then to the best universities, and then the best jobs at the best banks and the best consultancy firms, and in due course, they roll home in orderly fashion, with all the best salaries ... and the process begins all over again.

Question is: does it matter? Do we really want our own children to join them on their joyless trudge through life's to-do lists? I'm not sure that I do. We all want our children to thrive – obviously. But there are a million ways to do that.

The Supers, lacking in imagination what they so feverishly make up for in cash and efficiency, only understand the One. Their children will grow up rich and efficient. Twenty years hence, over their Christmas Day/Thanksgiving lunches, with massively ornate and often fairly disgusting veg accomps, they will feel, at least I hope so, reasonably comfortable in one another's company. And that, in the end, is probably what it's all about. For all of us. Let them eat their efficiently ornate veg accomps! We'll eat the cake! What do we care?

For all the money and effort and micro-management that goes into their upbringing, there isn't much evidence that the Superprogeny, with its Grade 8 trombone, its BAFTA Gold Standard Plus in inter-school trampolining, and its first-class degree in Geography at Cambridge ... is any more contented than the rest of us. Nor any more beloved ... Nor (and this bloody well has to count for something) making any more of a contribution to the health, beauty, wisdom or gaiety of our shared universe.

As for their SuperSuper Supermummies: rich, bossy, tunnel-visioned, magnificently absurd ... they're literally *pumping* their cash into the economy, while simultaneously giving us all something to snigger at on the way home from the school gate. And along the way (to be fair) they're probably doing quite a good job, as they hurl their bossy complaints at our children's teachers, of keeping the lazier ones on their toes.

Bless them. Giggle, snort. Pass the Port-and-Riesling-braised traditional red cabbage with smoked pancetta and roasted chestnuts. If you can. Without barfing.

What's not to love?

## Celebrity Mothers – On 'Snapping Back'

Madonna had a baby on 11 August 2000 and released an album called *Music*, five weeks later, on 19 September. I know the dates because I just Googled them. Obviously. Also because I had a baby at almost exactly the same time. And I remember, a few weeks after mine was born, sweating it out in a gym somewhere, en route to 'snapping back' into pre-pregnancy shape, and watching a video of Madonna dancing to her newly released song. Cool as a cucumber, she was, dressed in a Western-style shirt, buttoned tight across (no matter how closely I squinted, and believe me, I did) a *completely flat* belly ... How had she done it? Either she had made the video many months previously, before she was pregnant. OR she cheated. OR she was an alien.

However she had achieved it, her belly was flat, whereas mine was still a long way from it; and I can't pretend it wasn't vaguely dispiriting.

Celeb-watching always is, though, isn't it? Until celebs come a cropper, found dead in a bathtub under a million barbiturates, they are supposed to make the rest of us feel cumbersome, dragged down, in our parallel universe, by silly things like time, money, gravity and fat. It's what makes them fascinating ... -ish. Quite fascinating. More interesting than they would otherwise be.

Anyway, *apparently* (I read somewhere), most of these hospital-fresh superstar new mothers we see photographed on red carpets, stick-thin and grinning like banshees, have undergone tummy-tuck operations before they even exited the maternity ward. Is it true? Could easily be. And honestly, who can blame them? Their livelihood depends on being abnormally alluring. And there will always be plenty of abnormally alluring women out there, *without* post-baby bellies, only too ready to trip down the red carpet in their place. The poor things are under a lot more pressure than the rest of us.

It's just a bit annoying when they claim their freakishly svelte new figures are down to 'running around after baby' and a bit of breastfeeding. (Which Madonna didn't, by the way. And if you want to see the most embarrassing piece of television ever made, watch Vanessa Feltz on YouTube attempting to make girl-chat with a magnificently snooty Madonna by confiding her difficulties with getting a baby to 'latch on'. )

Please watch it. It's agonising.


## *Celebrity Mothers – On The Joys Of Motherhood*

'The greatest gift I can imagine is just the fact that I get to be his mom ...' (Jewel)

'I'm just filled to the brim with gratitude.' (Pink)

'I love my job but I love being a mum even more.' (Kate Winslet. To the Queen. Weirdly.)

'I'm so grateful I am my sons' mother.' (Rikki Lake)

'As a working mother high heels don't really fit into my life any more – but in a totally wonderful way. I would much rather think about my son than myself.'
(Sarah Jessica Parker)

'I thank God every day for giving me the opportunity to parent.'
(Maria Shriver)

Christ. Makes you want to sicky-burp though, doesn't it? It may be part of the star-status job description – as discussed – to float through the glamour universe making saccharine-sweet protestations about the joys of motherhood. But that doesn't stop it from being irritating. Not so much because of the mind-numbing banality, to which I think all celeb-watchers have to be inured simply to survive. But what a blast of fresh air it would be if, just once, couched somewhere amid the slavish orgas!gush: ('When your kids come home, they don't necessarily want to talk to you. They just want to know you're standing there, ready to talk.' Yeah. And thanks a bunch for that, seventeen-times-Oscar-nominee, Meryl Streep) ... there was instead just a teeny, tiny little pinch of sisterly honesty. For example:

I thank God everyday that I have a separate, high-status life of my own, into which I can always escape, when being 'Just a Mum' (standing at home, ignored but ready to be talked to) begins to feel a little soul-destroying ...

And I am truly filled to the brim with gratitude that sometimes I can just piss off and leave the baby with the nanny.

## Mumgelicals And Orgasimums

Like so many extreme groups, they make a lot more noise than their small numbers justify. Mumgelicals and Orgasimums can sometimes be confused, due to their equal propensity for placing Motherhood on the same, gravity-defying pedestal of sanctimony and sugar. But where Orgasimums are merely excessively sentimental (perhaps not the sharpest pencils in the box), Mumgelicals are downright *mean*. Often university-educated, bellicose and full of righteous, misogynist rage ... for their own safety and for the safety of all who come in contact with them, they should wipe the baby sick off their shoulders, swap the ponytail for a trip to the hair salon, dump the diaper bag, take a *long*, cool shower, and return to the workforce posthaste.

Enough of this. I get so irritated by type-of-mother generalisations and here I am falling into the same lazy trap.

Moving on then, to something more absorbing. I can't believe I've held out this long ...

## Sex

I think of those pathetic Victorian women with their twenty-five children each, half of whom didn't survive beyond the first year of life – and I am filled with pity, for sure: almost as much as I am filled with wonder. *How did they manage it?* We all know getting pregnant isn't nearly as easy as we claim it is to our teenage children. Those crazy Victorians must have been at it, shagging like bunny rabbits by the candlelight, night after night, year in and year out.

We tell each other so many lies about how often we have sex: when, why, how satisfactorily and with whom ... Nevertheless, it's a truth universally acknowledged that modern parents of young children don't shag each other that often. It's for all sorts of reasons, and we can say it's because 'the kids might walk in' until we are blue in the face, but, as many will recall from their dim and distant past, where there's a will, there tends to be a way.

Mostly, let's face it, exhausted from all that overwork and over-parenting, modern parents just don't fancy each other that much. Fair enough. *But how on earth,* with their lack of dimmer switches, central heating and en-suite bathroom facilities, in their perma-pregnant states, and with such an abundance of uncomfortable corsets, *how on earth* did the Victorians manage to keep the fires of marital desire burning?

There's only one satisfactory answer, at any rate only one that I can come up with: since women weren't meant to enjoy the sex anyway, a man could presumably expect to get his end away without even the most basic levels of effort or charm being expended. Which means ... that not only did nineteenth-century men often sport prodigious quantities of unattractive facial hair, they were *also* lousy lovers! Thank goodness they're all dead.

No use being angry about it now of course. Marriage in the bodice-ripping era was nothing more than a badly lit lifetime of mundane sexual abuse – or sex endured – the like of which possibly doesn't feature in *Fifty Shades of Grey*. Pity the Victorian women.

But actually never mind them. What about us? What about modern mothers?

Something happens between couples when they've spent too many of their leisure hours saying to each other:

'Has he done a poo today?'

'Have I got puke on my back?'

'But you went to the gym yesterday, it's my turn.'

Interspersed with:

'Are my tits leaking?'

'But I changed him last time.'

'No. No! Not like that. No, oh God ... it doesn't matter. Forget it. I'll do it.'

... A little of the magic fades away ... How could it not?

When children are very young, parents can sometimes feel like zoo animals, pacing our baby-safe cages: bound together by pastel-coloured plastics, feeding routines, sugary-smelling nappy wipes – and a wretched shortage of funds. It's hard, from time to time, not to mistake our fellow cellmate for a jailer.

It's a dreadful state of affairs, and actually I think it's a credit to the entire human race that so many partnerships survive at all. You've been breathing the same air, negotiating the same chores all day. Add to that – yes, there is the constant threat of a child barging in on the act ... and what with one thing another, pandas in captivity spring to mind. And I'm not sure there's much of a way round it, at least not in the early years, when childcare is so demanding that even a trip to the lavatory requires negotiation and pre-planning.

No matter how much you loved and fancied each other once – and may yet again – for the moment at least, the chances are that you are each other's anti-aphrodisiac.

You're just not that into each other.

In the meantime, there's Daddy Porn on the laptop and Mummy Porn on the Kindle … And there's the painful question, never to be answered explicitly:

If neither party much wants to have sex with the other, is it reasonable or sensible to insist, along with all the other restrictions their shared situation necessarily imposes, that they don't at least entertain the idea of having sex with someone else?

I'm not advocating open relationships. Holy Cow and God forbid! I'm just not, *not* advocating them, either … Perhaps the traditional Upper Class/French, loose-reined approach: of tact, discretion and pragmatism … has something to recommend it after all.

Human love doesn't package neatly. Will never package like it does in the ads. And no matter how high we build our walls of baby-safe plastic, we are still human. A nuclear family consists of a collection of individuals, thrown together, to a degree; mutually dependent and fundamentally loving. But nothing is perfect. Love is nuanced and complicated, and – if it was ever true at all – a lot more robust than perhaps we give it credit for.

Have I gone too far? Have I lost you?

Awww, *shucks*. Well, we can't agree on everything.

**DAISY WAUGH**

## *'Sexualisation' Of Children*

Children look preposterous when they strut about in adult clothing, copying the dance moves they've watched on TV. Then again, the pop stars look pretty preposterous themselves: adult women, often in silly clothes, mouthing meaningless words, grinding their hips into thin air and gazing with indiscriminate longing at every one of us: you and me and Bob and Derek and Samantha. At least, when children mimic them, they tend to realise they look absurd.

Aside from that minor point, there is the other, less comfortable one which, in our ever more puritanical and sentimental approach to childhood, I think we are sometimes prone to overlook: that most children are never wholly unsexual in any case. I could provide a long, embarrassing list of people I had crushes on from about the age of seven. It starts with little Mark Lester, of *Oliver Twist* fame, with whom I was truly infatuated. And it includes the Bionic Woman.

Maybe it's a natural response to the guilt, confusion and disappointment we feel for our drably sexualised modern world, but as adults we tend increasingly to exaggerate not just the sexual purity of our children but the value of that purity, too.

A friend of mine was taken aside by his eight-year-old daughter's teacher not long ago because his daughter's friend had reported to her mother that he had used 'sexual language inappropriately, referring to his male body parts' in her presence, and the mother had lodged a complaint with the school

He'd hit his thumb, hammering a nail into the kitchen wall while the girls were eating tea at the kitchen table, and shouted, 'Penis!'

Which I call a fairly moderate response.

Now when he goes to fetch his daughter from school, on the occasions he can bring himself to visit the school at all, he walks with an imaginary DIRTY FILTHY PERVERT sign hanging around his neck.

I am often amazed by parents' knee-jerk prissiness when it comes to their children's exposure to any aspect of sex, and yet who feel relatively untroubled by their exposure to the sort of pow-pow, thump-in-the-chops, kick-in-the head violence we see on TV every day. I feel the exact opposite. I loathe violence and infuriate my children by endlessly switching it off, or yelling at them to block their ears and close their eyes until it's over. Violence, it seems to me, is always loathsome. But sex is part of who we are; it's one of the better aspects (or can be) of being human ... And *maybe* if we weren't so squeamish about it, modern sexual appetites wouldn't be so fucked up, so dependent for fulfilment on hyper-real super-plastic body shapes and lonely, screen-delivered panto-style sex shows.

Ho hum. Perhaps that's enough of this kitchen-sink psychology. The point is – think back! Have you really forgotten? Children, by nature, never *are* quite the innocent little earthworms we like to pretend. And it seems to me that our frantic attempts to shield them – and ourselves – from this uncute but immutable fact of human life, only makes things more difficult for all of us, as well as significantly reducing the number of films we can all watch together.

## *Mummy Porn*

Irritating, isn't it, when they call it that. As opposed to what? *Lady* Porn? *Girl* Porn? *Barren Woman* Porn? *Opted Not To Have Children* Porn? *Never Got Round To It And Now it's Too Late* Porn?

Put 'Mummy' in front of anything and it tends to suck out any possible element of threat. So it's patronising. On the other hand, annoyingly, it may also be quite apt.

Of all the ladies, girls and the women-without-children (and from the way fulfilled motherhood and fully-realised-womanliness are equated, we might be forgiven for considering childless women hardly women at all), it's likely that Mummies are in need of porn the most. They're so busy lactating into electronic milking machines, handcrafting hats for the Year Three Easter Bonnet Parade, cooking menu options for their children's wheat-intolerant 'play dates' and squabbling with their other half about whose turn it is to empty the nappy disposal unit ... the chances are high they're not getting much of the real McCoy.

Added to which Mummies are so busy being *nice*, burying their sexuality under that sweet-natured Mummy-Moo, they're probably most in need of something truly extra filthy, if only to add a little grit to the daily syrup.

A lot of feminists get their panties in a wedge because so much of Mummy Porn is about subjugation. But I don't see why it matters. Sexual fantasies are only that. Fantasies. Separate from real life, where – in the civilised world at least – men and women are free to function as equals, if they want.

For lack of a milkman to invite in – and unfortunately these days not everyone has access to a milkman (ask your GP for a leaflet), why not unwedge those panties, lie back and Enjoy.

## Love 'n' Subjugation

What's a bit of sex play between lovers? It may, in the cold light of day, seem entirely absurd, but then almost everything about sex seems pretty absurd when you're not in the mood for it.

Far more insidious, because it affects the way we live (and with apologies for the tub-thumping, I know I've made this point before), is the confusion between love and subjugation, which is intrinsic to modern martyr-style mothering. *That's* what ought to be getting our knick-knacks in a tangle.

## Mums In TV Advertisements

Freak me out. Are they talking to *anyone* out there?

## Moms In American TV Advertisements

Make me despair. America, after all, is home to (why yes, among others) probably the most evolved, most egalitarian, most socially advanced people in the world. How do they put up with it? I love America. So long as I never switch on the TV.

## 2 Cs In A K

How the admen sometimes refer to those set-piece TV commercials featuring happy mums in domestic settings, sharing their exorbitant pleasure over a new household product.

Two Cunts In A Kitchen.

Isn't that nice?

## Mumsnet

We're told it's very powerful: so powerful it can topple governments; so powerful that when prime minister of the day Gordon Brown failed to reveal his favourite biscuit during a Mumsnet live web chat, all hell broke loose on the nation's front pages. So powerful, in fact, that the last general election was briefly referred to as the 'Mumsnet election', after politicians got it into their heads that the nation's 'Mums' might all be persuaded to vote the same way. If only the correct favourite biscuit could be chosen.

... There's something about the idea of Mumsnet that irritates as many women as it pleases. The idea of it certainly irritates me. It's not just the name (don't call me 'Mum'), it's the suggestion that 'mums' per se, by the mere fact of being 'mums', are likely to have interests and values in common.

However, a person can't write a book about modern motherhood without at least checking it out. I suppose. And although I know only a few women who admit to having visited the site, it claims to get over 40 million hits a month. So we have to assume that somebody out there, other than Gordon Brown and his unusual wife Sarah, must at least be checking in from time to time.

Duty called. And to be fair, the website is not as chock-a-block with Mumgelicals and Orgasimums as I had imagined. Brimming with platitudinous advice, yes, but not half as sanctimonious as its biscuity public image might suggest.

... My whistlestop visit probably wasn't enhanced by the fact that most of the exchanges in their chat room ('the country's most popular meeting place for parents', according to Mumsnet's home page) seem to have been written in code. Mumsnet Mums communicate with one another in a whole lexicon of acronyms incomprehensible to the rest of the world:

'DP really hates the idea of being away from family during the week.'

'We were in the same situation a year ago and DH ended up dropping so many balls he got fired.'

'DH left 5 a.m. Monday morning, back Thursday night. Would be different now with DC.'

'If you're an SAHM, try to get as much work done as possible during the week. You have to work on your relationships as well as family life IME ...'

No doubt I could break the code if I could be bothered. But I have to admit – duty didn't call for quite long enough to try.

I understand Mumsnet may serve a helpful, even valuable purpose, in that it may help to connect mothers of very small children who might otherwise feel horribly isolated. I also understand it involves itself in much more than politicians' biscuits. And above all, I understand that it's not (it could never be) half as smug as its public image. Bit even so, something rankles about being asked to see anything at all – except my own children – through the prism of my maternity.

Mumsnet is not for me ☹ .

But HEY! ... That must be because not *all MUMS are the same!*


## Don't Call Me 'Mum'

It happens when the first ward nurse approaches the hospital bedside. 'Mum' (for on this occasion it was *moi*) may be too bamboozled at that early landing in Mumland to think too much about it, beyond a vague observation that the ward nurse is a little rude.

The nurse may not even bother to glance at Mum (it was *moi*). She may only have eyes for Mum's baby.

'Mum,' she will say. 'Do you want to pop Baby on the bed for me, so I can take a quick look at him?'

'... pop Baby on the bed *for me*,' she says.

What? For *Nurse Bobbit*, employed by the state to check all the babies as they come into the ward, day after day after day?

Or for *me*? AKA Mum (for it was *moi*), who stands before Nurse Bobbit and has a name, and who works and pays her taxes, and who loves her beautiful, healthy baby far better than

Nurse Bobbit ever will. What *folie de grandeur* to suggest that Nurse Bobbit is looking at my baby, not for my baby's benefit, or for mine, but for hers! What lousy manners!

It doesn't matter. A tiny scene, involving one careless nurse, a little too quick to patronise; one blissed-out, hormone-addled Mum (for it was *moi*) and one perfectly beautiful, healthy Baby. Who cares?

I didn't care, and I still don't. Except, you have to ask: *what just happened*?

It was to be the first of many, many times I would be addressed by a fellow adult, not as an individual, but as a biological relationship to another one. And even now, after all these years, it takes me aback each time it happens.

There are only three people in the world who can call me Mum, and they know who they are. To anyone else: call me fatso for all I care. Call me anything at all.

Just don't call me Mum. I am not your Mum. If I were, you'd have better manners.

# PART 2

# PREGNANCY & BIRTH

*(Do Not Last For Ever)*

If you've read this far and not already posted your letter bomb, you hardly need to be warned. The following few sections – Pregnancy and Birth, Babycare and Childcare – divided loosely into the three chronological stages of motherhood (those stages that I have so far experienced), are most adamantly not intended as a guide. They are far from foolproof. In fact, they are not for fools at all. I don't aim to offer answers, more to throw into the morass of wastefulness, blandness, sentimentality and neurotic hyperactivity, a handful of pragmatic suggestions and a few long-overdue questions.

And no, of course it doesn't speak for everyone. I only speak from my own experience as a modern, educated, middle-class woman, who is more truculent than most (perhaps), especially when expected to jump through what may seem to others as harmless enough hoops. I just don't think they *are* harmless. That's the point. They achieve nothing, they waste our living time, they encourage us to lacquer our lives with bullshit. And the simpering demeans us.

There has never been a moment (I will add, once again) when I wasn't grateful to be a mother, but there have been many moments when I have felt bewildered and alienated by society's inflexible expectations of me 'as a mother'. And the guilt I felt, at my failure to feel as blandly fulfilled as I knew I was meant to feel, only intensified the sense of isolation.

So. Here is this.

Some potentially liberating observations for Mothers (and Future Mothers) who might sometimes find themselves feeling the same way.

## Baby On Board

I presume everyone (except for the people who put them up there) finds those 'Baby On Board' bumper stickers irritating. Sentimental, self-important, and potentially even self-defeating, they assume that on spotting said fatuous sticker and learning of 'Baby', the driver coming up behind will take extra care as a result. But why? With or without stickers, most people don't tend to want to drive into each other. The 'baby on board' may be beloved of the car-sticker owner, but not especially so of the stranger driving the car behind, who – we have to assume – will be doing his level best to avoid a collision in any case. He hardly requires an added incentive.

Never mind. It doesn't matter. One of life's minor irritations, nothing more. But it makes one ponder on the narrow thought processes of the person who went to the bother of putting the sticker there in the first place.

Also, by the way, it's worth noting (since I may not be the only one on whom it has this effect), that the sight of such a sticker on the back of a car often makes me want to career up its tailpipe, honking loudly. Only because I feel sorry for the baby, being landed with such disturbingly self-important and solipsistic parents, and feel duty-bound to try to make the poor thing smile. For once in its bubble-wrapped life.

So watch out.

The Baby On Board badges sometimes seen on the coat lapels of pregnant commuters, on the other hand, are more poignant. Also, unlike the car stickers, they serve a function. Worn in hope that a fellow passenger might offer them a seat, their wearers have my fullest sympathy and support. And also gratitude. How many times have you looked at a woman's swollen belly and exhausted face, and wondered: is she or isn't she? Should I be sitting while she is standing, or is she just having a tired, fat day?

A friend of mine was having a tired, fat day a few years back, and some well-meaning person offered her a seat on the Tube. It was, she says, one of the most mortifying moments of her adult life. (On the other hand, at around the same time and at the grand old age of 41, she was also asked to produce formal ID at the Tesco checkout before they would sell her any alcohol. So let's contain our grief.) The point is, with a Baby On Board badge, we all know where we are. Nobody fat gets unnecessarily offended. And with a bit of luck, nobody pregnant has to stand.

You don't spot the badges often. Or I certainly don't. But the odd, rare sighting makes me long to do more than simply offer my seat. I want to throw my arms around the badge owner and tell her, just in case she's forgotten, which she may have done because I often did, *that pregnancy passes.* Also, in case she's forgotten, or doesn't know it yet, that the exquisite moment at the end of it all, the moment it leads up to, when the baby is in your arms at last, out and about, and alive and kicking, makes every long and lonely, mad and miserable month of its gestation worthwhile.

Obviously I wouldn't actually do it. No. That would be irritating. And I might be arrested. Also, she might actually be quite happy, pregnant. Some women like it. Apparently. I've heard them talking sometimes, on TV and radio.

But, my goodness, for the rest of us – for *most* of us, dare I suggest? – and with a million apologies to those women who are struggling to get pregnant, and with a million hidden parentheses regarding my own wonder and gratitude for having managed it at all, let's never pretend that being pregnant is fun. It is, on the whole, a drawn-out and dismal experience. From the moment the first symptom kicks in. From the moment you tell the first person your happy news, and they grin at you, and speak a little louder and a little more clearly, to tell you how you must be feeling: *YOU MUST BE THRILLED …*

Or no: from long before that day … Well, now. Gosh. Where to start?

From the bit where you start feeling sick?

Or before that? Before you even suspect you're pregnant.

When you begin, inexplicably, to feel a little out of sync, a little angry. And tearful. And mad. And argumentative. And hungry. And fat. And inexplicably low. And inexplicably high. And inexplicably, ferociously bad-tempered.

Not everybody feels all of the above, all of the time. Apparently. Even if they do, please understand I am not suggesting the process isn't worth it. To win such an excellent prize is likely to command extreme levels of inconvenience and pain. Yes, yes, *yes*. Fair enough. Nevertheless.

Being pregnant is quite difficult enough. It's made more difficult and a far lonelier and madder journey by the bland, conformist refusal to acknowledge what a peculiarly isolating and disconcerting process it actually is.

Baby on Board? YOU MUST BE THRILLED!

And yes, you very probably do feel thrilled. Absolutely thrilled. Among a million other emotions.

'How are you feeling?' people ask warmly. But it's rhetorical. Nice girls pull a little face. 'Ooh, a teeny bit sick!' they say. Little face. 'But *really well* otherwise! Really, really well!'

If I ruled the world, I would rewrite those Baby On Board badges and hand them out, free, with every pregnancy testing kit ever sold. And they would read something like this:

Sick, miserable, exhausted, angry, frightened, lonely, lost, incredibly emotional, horribly needy, fatter than usual, struggling with loss of my 'erotic capital', unable to drown sorrows in usual manner, paralysingly exhausted – and suffering from a major identity crisis. But ABSOLUTELY THRILLED ABOUT THE BABY, OKAY? Please, before I embarrass myself and everyone here by a random attack of pointless but strangely soothing sobbing, *give me your seat*!

Not everyone would appreciate the leaflets of course. Lest we forget: some women really like being pregnant. Apparently.

Bully for them.

## *Being Public Property*

Late on in one of my pregnancies, I ventured into an unusually smart cheese shop, where a deferential middle-aged sales assistant, male, with a belly about the same size as mine, insisted on helping me make my cheese choices. I wished he wouldn't but there – that's what you get in smart cheese shops. No peace.

Anyway, I ordered some Cheddar. Boring old Cheddar. Specifically because I could smell his bossiness above all the Pont l'Évêques and Camemberts, and I knew he was longing, perhaps more than he had longed to do anything in a very long time, to lecture me about the dangers of mixing pregnant women and soft cheeses. And I didn't want to get into that conversation. So I said:

'Could I please have some of that Cheddar?'

Over his own big fat belly, he gazed at mine. I found it vaguely intrusive. Thought I'd buy the Cheddar and get the hell out of there, before he suggested feeling the baby kick. He said, 'Actually, madam, we really don't recommend it … '

'Recommend what?' I asked. Snarled. Possibly.

'I'm aware that doctors only tend to warn pregnant ladies about *soft* cheeses. But I prefer to play it safe. And I personally don't recommend this particular Cheddar cheese to pregnant ladies. As I say to all my pregnant lady customers, "It's better safe than sorry …"' He paused, looked unbearably smug, and before I had time to lamp him, added, 'Apologies if you think I'm fussing. But Baby may thank you for it later!'

He was trying to be kind. Perhaps. It was harmless enough. Maybe he was just trying to break up the monotony of a long, cheese-selling day. In any case, he could never have guessed quite how angry it would make me. And perhaps if he had said it four months earlier, it would have simply dropped into the general swill of Irritating and Unsolicited Pregnancy Advice offered up by people who don't even fucking know you ... I might have been able to smile in a saintly manner and rise above it. But his comments, his infuriating assumption that I needed his advice, the insinuation that my unborn baby was in some way as much his responsibility as it was mine, all came at the end of nine months of being on the receiving end of the same: personal comments, uninvited commentary, unwanted and unneeded instructions.

So I left the shop. Without the Cheddar. And blubbed with rage all the way home.

### *Things To Avoid When Pregnant*
*(Aside From The Fat Man In The Posh Cheese Shop)*

hair dye
hot baths
soft cheeses
cured hams
shellfish
too much standing
lying flat

getting angry

aromatherapy

cycling

steam rooms

being over 35

marijuana

being fat

being thin

illegal drugs

paint

mackerel

reaching up for things

computer screens (CRT type)

inhaling washing powder

junk food

running

too much sitting

vitamin A supplements

X-rays

tennis

sun beds

ticks

lifting things

microwaves

aspirin

tuna

hot dogs

reptiles

sea bass

new mattresses

lawn sprays

salmon

horse riding

dog shit

soft-boiled eggs

amusement park rides

dog saliva

contact sports

flea collars

red meat

tap water

paint thinner

cleaning products

electric blankets

smoking

pâté

alcohol

passive smoking

bad thoughts

salami

coffee

high heels

tea

cat litter

peanuts

the soles of your feet

mayonnaise

stress

pop concerts
water beds ...


The trouble is of course, in the bottomless trough of impractical and officious precautions, it's difficult to know what advice is worth attending to and what can be happily discarded. By Baby Number 3, I ignored pretty much all of it. Which isn't to say I went out of my way to breathe in pesticides. But I didn't go out of my way *not* to breathe them in, either. And sometimes – yep – when the initial morning sickness had passed (when even the thought of it made me want to be sick), *I smoked cigarettes.*


With Baby Number 1, I wasn't so confident of course. Added to which, I was genuinely worried: the baby had not been planned and was conceived during a period of heavy-duty partying, in the course of which, m'lud, a quantity of unhealthful materials had been ingested.

I felt I had to ask a doctor about it, just in case the damage I feared I had unknowingly wrought on my unborn child might yet be rectified in some way. Nevertheless, I was terrified. I envisaged the doctor, inputting my sad confession into that giant computer ... making an emergency call to social services as soon as I left the surgery. I envisaged council officers with weighing machines and measuring sticks coming to my house ... placing the baby on a watch list of infants born to 'unfit' mothers, liable to be removed by the authorities at any time.

So I confided my worries, listing my drinks with head hanging. (Forgive me, Father, for I have sinned.) 'But you have to understand. It was before I realised I was ... ' The GP, bless her, burst out laughing. She was not your run-of-the-mill materno-Nazi doc, but a kind and reasonable human being, and one to whom I am eternally grateful (I won't name her, or the Mumgelicals will be sending her letter bombs, too). 'Never say I said so,' she told me, 'but as a rule of thumb, if it's the very early days, a foetus will either survive no matter what you chuck at it – booze, drugs and everything else ... or it was going to die anyway. And if your baby has survived, as it obviously has, you have absolutely nothing to worry about. Don't give it another thought.'

I am not a doctor, and obviously I am not advocating binges of any kind – before, during or after conception. Nor at any other time. *Duh.* In any case, it's none of my business. I am simply passing on something I was told by a doctor who was kind enough, and brave enough, to pass it on to me. Because it's something we have every right to know.

Foetus Danger does *not* lurk at every corner. Far from it. Which is why the world population has more than doubled in fifty years. Pregnancy would be a lot more relaxing if we could only be encouraged to remember that.

## Shopping For Baby

It was always slightly depressing, in the old days, when friends and siblings started having their own families. A bit like when they give up smoking; you feel like you've lost them to the Other Side. As indeed, in many ways, you have. When I confided to one close girlfriend, who at the time had no children of her own, that I, too, was abandoning her for the badlands – or the blandlands – she grinned dutifully, said, 'Congratulations' and paused to think of something else to add. 'It's a fantastic new retail opportunity.'

Quite funny. Or I thought it was back then. But the joke wears thin pretty quickly, does it not? A fantastic 'Retail Opportunity' it may be – for the retailers. An expectant mother (especially first time round), all ajitter with nerves and untried beliefs and goofy idealism, is nothing if she isn't ripe for the fleece.

Wander the aisles of the dreaded Mothercare and the truth of this soon becomes clear. A truly craven New World opens up; a world that seems to be made only of germs and fear and sharp corners and worry: of bumping and burning, spilling and choking, slipping and tripping hazards, none of which had been previously considered, and yet every one of which (it transpires) could be avoided with another piece of pastel-coloured plastic and a just few extra £££. What price, after all, your baby's health and safety?

It's been a few years since I have needed to venture down those baby kit shelves. But I've just returned from examining the fare at John Lewis in London's Oxford Street, and I see that, unsurprisingly, nothing much has changed. If anything, it has got worse … Was there, for example, a Miniland Thermoadvanced Plus thermometer available (£50), with an 'ultra-fast: one-second' heart rate reading, a clock with 'time and date display', a 'high/low temperature indicator' and a 'voice messaging facility' – when I was last shopping for Babygros? And if not, how did my babies ever survive without it?

And had they invented that peculiar-looking dummy, with the grisly old-man-gusset-netting sewn into one end, so that 'baby' could suck on whatever was inside it without danger of choking to death... ? Honestly, I think not.

I'm finished with this stage of family life, thankfully, and I am pleased to report that despite the lack of any chew-safe gusset arrangements, all three children emerged from their babyhood intact. This afternoon, with all the baby-related terrors having receded, I looked at the shelves of pastel crap being offered for sale to nervous mothers – and laughed in disbelief. The cynicism, the fearmongering, the emotional blackmail, the bullshit and the sheer fatuous, vacuous wastefulness are all truly breathtaking! How was I ever taken in?

Take the 'Doidy Cup' as one small example. Sold in shades of baby-friendly colours at Britain's favourite shop (and no doubt elsewhere), it's a plastic cup with a 'uniquely slanted' rim, designed, it explains on the pack, to encourage babies to drink from a rim rather than a spout ... The 'natural action' of which (what does that even *mean?*) 'encourages good oral movements'. As opposed to 'bad oral movements'? Saying 'Fuck' in front of a member of the NHS Home Visitor team? ... 'Health professionals promote the DOIDY CUP', it continues in its child-friendly scrawl, 'to help prevent long-term health problems ... including: tooth decay, speech problems, poor chewing skills, poor feeding, anaemia, failure to thrive ... '

*Failure to thrive?!? It's a plastic cup.* With a slanted rim.

So. One afternoon, a month or so before our firstborn was due, the baby's father and I arranged to meet at a large branch of the spirit-sapping Hell that is Mothercare, to stock up on whatever baby-soothing, hazard-avoiding equipment we might discover we needed.

It was – remember – the first baby. We were excited. We travelled to Mothercare with quite a spring in our steps. But at the first soft sound of the tinkly-winkly store music, something like stage fright, mixed with claustrophobia – and horror – seemed to overcome us both. We didn't articulate it, so far as I remember. But this drippy, tinkly-winkly world was quite alien to us, as it must be to any adults. It seemed to suck the oxygen from our lungs ... the blood from our veins ... the spirit from our very souls ...

Aye.

We must have spent an hour or two wandering those aisles, listening to that God-awful music, picking up Anywayup Cups, 'suction bowl trainer plates' and packs of nipple-shaped dummies, perfect for newborns (*Who'd've thought, eh?*) ... We emerged a lifetime later, the early dawn of awareness chilling our bones. This then was the pastel-coloured world we would be inhabiting henceforth, and from which (with luck) there would be no turning back.

We had spoken to no one in the shop and bought nothing except, in desperation because I couldn't leave completely empty-handed, a small, cotton caterpillar with a bell in the tail. I left it on the bus on the journey home.

## What Not To Buy

According to the manufacturers of the Thudguard® Wear-Anywhere Infant Safety Hat, 'Over 318,575 baby & toddler head injuries are recorded each year in the UK alone'!

Should we be worried? You bet!

Fortunately, though, for £21.99 plus p&p, Thudguard® has come up with just the solution. The product is available in 45 countries, and the company has recently celebrated selling its millionth helmet. Here's the ad. Top up on tranquillisers and breathe a sigh of relief. Because thanks to the foresight of Thudguard®, everything's going to be okay.

---

Thudguard®

It's normal for young children to sustain bumps and bruises occasionally as part of exploring. However, learning to walk in a world of hard surfaces can turn a special moment into a heart-rending incident in a flash. Consider for one moment being the height of an average toddler. If you're not sure about this, get down on your hands and knees and have a wander around. Look at all the furniture and hard surfaces you would hit if you fell – both inside your home and outside in your garden.

Now imagine you have wobbly legs, you're only just finding your balance and you fall over more than you'd like to, because you're just learning to walk. Remember learning to ride a bicycle or learning to ice-skate for the first time?

What are the chances of you falling over and hitting something solid? Most homes today have hardwood floors or tiles so statistically the chances are really high. The problem is this kind of fall is very common in even the safest homes and gardens. The damage to a falling toddler's hands and knees can be an acceptable form of pain for learning but a head injury can be traumatic for both infant and parent. Thudguard® goes one step further and takes the protection straight to the infant's head, giving you great peace of mind.

---

Thudguard®s are reasonably new. In fact, they were recently featured on *The Apprentice*. I heard about them through a friend who founded a bunch of babywear shops, and who – to her eternal credit – was sufficiently appalled by their existence that she refused to stock them in her stores. (See? Not all purveyors of baby kit are completely cynical.) ... And I would plug her stores here – except she hardly needs it. Her stores don't treat mothers like neurotic, half-baked children and they don't treat children like precious china gods. And consequently (I like to think) they are thriving.

But I digress.

Of all the things that did actually exist when my children were babies, that I was advised to buy but never needed – all the hideous pastel bits of overpriced plastic junk, the germ alert sprays, the noise alert intercoms, the nursing chairs and changing units, the baby door stoppers and the baby cupboard locks, the 'baby aid' first aid kits, the soft-glow safety night lights ... The thing I most resent having invested in is the electric breast pump. I resent it for reasons far beyond the money wasted. In fact I resent it so much it has its own separate entry in this book.

But, aside from the breast pump (and the Thudguard®), here, in ascending order, are ten of the most useless bits of baby-related junk currently available to waste your money on. Most of which I myself have bought at some point, and immediately regretted, and all of which, by Baby Number 3, I survived very easily without.

**10) Stair gates**. An early-warning hallway greeting statement to all newcomers that the adults in charge:
**a)** don't understand their chief function as parents – to teach children as quickly and efficiently as possible how best to survive in an adult world. Toddlers who find themselves untended at the top of a stairway may well take a tumble. And, unless they're very stupid, will remember to take better care around tops of stairways in the future.
**b)** don't know how to close doors behind them,
**c)** lack any sense of an aesthetic,
**d)** have officially ceded control of their environment. The lunatics have taken over the asylum.
Proud to say – mostly because of the DIY required to install them – our household never succumbed.

**9) A nappy changing unit**. Thought I wanted this, first time round, but couldn't afford it. Used the bed, and … weirdly … it worked just fine.

**8) An electric bottle warmer**. Used a microwave.
But Laydies! DO TAKE CARE.
*Experts don't recommend it.* Leaving aside any yet-to-be-

proven, possible-microwave-associated health risks, <u>please do remember</u> that things put in microwaves can get *ever so hot*! If you feel unsure, ask your GP for a leaflet.

And don't forget, IF YOU DO FEEL CONCERNED about using a microwave ... you can always use a 'kettle'. Once again, however, you should be aware that these can sometimes get a bit ouchie, especially if the water inside has been allowed to 'boil'. As a rough guideline, if the water is 'bubbling' (bubbles rising to the surface), it's very likely to be 'scorching hot'. When handling a kettle (or any hot object), I generally advise Mums and Laydies to arm themselves with a good pair of rubber-insulated oven gloves.

7) **A nappy disposal unit**. It looked so hi-tech in the shop. I had imagined that for the appearance and price, there would be some sort of dustbin lorry-like trash-crushing effect hidden within the mechanism. But, hey – it turns out there wasn't any mechanism, hidden or otherwise. 'Nappy disposal units' are just bins – nothing more or less – with perfumed bin bags inside, which store the stinking nappies in a pointless, gag-inducing, perfumed-bin-bagged, stinking-nappy sausage chain ... until such a time as no more perfumed shit-packs can be squeezed within its slick and groovy lines and the chain has to be cut, the contraption emptied and the sausage chain of ageing shit has to be hauled downstairs to an alternative dustbin ... And it's quite surprising just how much one tiny baby's piss and shit can weigh, if you let it pile up in a slick-looking disposal unit for long enough.

Also, by the way, it begs the question: just how many shitty nappies does a person want to keep stored in perfumed shit bags inside a warm bedroom before even the idea of them, reeking away in their polythene sausage shape, makes everyone in the house think they're liable to die of typhoid any moment?

Moral of that tale? Not sure. Don't have babies, perhaps? Nappies, piss and shit will always be involved.

Or maybe, when tempted to buy an especially slick-looking bit of plastic from that pastel-coloured baby kit shelf: *move on.*

**6) A Tiny Tatty Teddy Pregnancy Journal**. Okay ... I didn't buy this. Nor did anyone I know. Nor, in fact, did I even know such a thing existed until about two hours ago ... I've just spotted it for sale in Argos. It's pastel pink and has a picture of two teddy bears cuddling one another on the cover—

Which is confusing, isn't it? Because the book isn't for 'Baby'! It's for 'Mum'! Who, despite fulfilling a biological function only possible for a mature woman, is often assumed to have mysteriously regressed, as a result of her impending motherhood, into a teddy-cuddling second infancy of her own. On the Tiny Tatty Teddy Journal sales blurb, it says:

*Nothing can compare to the joy of becoming a parent! This Tiny Tatty Teddy Journal will help you capture the memories made during the special time as you prepare yourself for your little bundle of joy. Your pregnancy journal will build into a precious keepsake, a permanent book of memories for you to cherish for ever!*

So cherish this:

Day 1: wake up, puke, blub, bicker, puke, blub, bicker – snooze.

Day 2: wake up, blub, puke, bicker, blub, bicker – snooze.

Day 3: blubpukewakeup, puke, blub, bicker – snooze.

As previously discussed, being pregnant isn't fun. It's bloody awful. A process to be got through. A means to an end. I think we can do without the keepsake.

**5) Any clothes made to fit newborn babies**, most especially Babygros, unless you're willing to take scissors to the foot ends. **Also, all baby clothes made of cashmere**. On a par with Prince Charles having a servant to put toothpaste on his toothbrush each night. If he ever did.

**4) A Moses basket**. Costs about £50 and lasts for a maximum of three months – after which, it's good for nothing at all. Too large for a beach bag. Too feeble to carry logs. Possibly good for a dry flower arrangement in the hallway – if there's room in the hallway among the rest of the baby clutter. Babies do look cute in them. No arguing with that. There again they tend to look cute anyway. Any time, any place, etc.

**3) A baby bath**. Another ugly piece of plastic, almost certainly pastel, probably embellished with drippy-looking teddy bears and, most unforgivable of all, too bulky to store anywhere. Everlastingly annoying and truly pointless. What's wrong with the sink?

**2) Thermometers**. For measuring the temperature of anything: rooms, baths ... (seriously, *who buys these things?*) even bodies. I've never understood the need for them. Nevertheless, for the sake of convention, along with egg cups and oven gloves, a body temperature thermometer is something I've been meaning to buy since – well, since Baby Number 1 arrived, back in 1997. I never have got round to it and I am beginning to accept now that it's unlikely I ever will. In any case, if somebody's burning up, they're burning up. It doesn't take the Surgeon General to spot when a child has a fever. What difference does it make, in the end, knowing the number on the temperature dial?

**1) A pram and/or Transformer-style pushchair** with pram add-on ... No matter with what high hopes it is acquired: no matter how much it costs, how groovy its colours, how snazzy its snap-'n'-go, click-'n'-run, twist-'n'-shout attachments, the sight of the thing will be depressing within a month. Rain-drenched, mud-spattered, with strangers' chewing gum stuck to the wheels and draped in hideous plastic baubles, it'll be blocking the hallway and driving everyone mad. That's all. The bigger it is, the more expensive it will be, and the higher the chance of householders stubbing their toe as they squeeze irritably by. And the more elaborate it is, the more of it there is to break, the more of it there is to store, and the more truly hateful the contraption will become.

I borrowed a second-hand, folding pushchair with a seat that partially reclined from the girl who now runs the baby shops ... The experts tell you that small babies mustn't use them because they need to lie flat, so I put in a pillow to flatten it. The end.

Total cost saved: impossible to say. Depends how mad you might have gone with the pram. Not far off a thousand quid? Maybe even more.

## (Wet) Dads In Antenatal Classes

I didn't attend many antenatal classes. For lots of reasons. Because I was busy doing other things. Because as far as the actual birth was concerned, I wanted to think about it as little as possible until the moment it was upon me ... Also, because during these classes there seemed to be an infuriating assumption that we were all the same, and therefore ought all to be thinking and feeling the same way about the process ahead.

Nevertheless, I did attend a handful – up until the class when we were due to sit in a happy circle and watch a baby's head emerging into the world on a big fat cinema screen above us. It's bad enough watching a live birth in a biology lesson at school, aged 13, when it all seems reasonably abstract, but to watch it with a round belly of your own, and in the company of a lot of soft-breathing, sympathetic Noddy-men – possibly in sandals – was more than I could manage.

The biological realities of birth, in case no one's noticed, are not terribly beautiful. They are a grisly and painful means to a beautiful end. Also, call me old-fashioned (as opposed, on this occasion, to thoroughly modern) but they're *private*. I don't want to discuss 'mucus plugs' with anyone, actually – ever. Unless I absolutely have to. But I really don't want to discuss them with a roomful of unknown men. Wet Dads, or otherwise. For men and women to remain reasonably alluring to one another – which must be an aim of sorts, mustn't it? because Mutual Attraction Can Be Fun (ask your GP for a leaflet) some details of our biological selves are better left unshared.

Love from

Joan Collins xx

And me.


## Fathers At The Birth

When our third came into the world, her father was sitting on a plastic chair in a corridor outside – almost certainly with a BlackBerry in his hand, and, (or so the midwife reported back, laughing her bosomy laugh) out for the count. Fast asleep. It was fine with me. To be brutal, he wasn't needed. Close by – for sure. But not in the room. As long as there were no complications, the process was something I preferred to get through with as few people witnessing it as possible.

Each to their own. I know a woman who, along with her husband, her best friend and her mother, also insisted on her *father* being present at the birth. It's a far cry from anything I would have wanted. But there you have it: we are all mad in different ways ... I find the current fervour for including Daddy in each and every stage of a process that is, after all, inescapably female, and in which he has no real role – contrary to say the least. And a little tactless.

After our second baby was born, the midwife asked if his father wanted to cut the umbilical cord.

'Probably not,' I giggled.

The midwife shot me a malevolent look (and after all we'd been through together!).

'I wasn't asking you,' she said primly, pushing her grisly tools towards him. 'I was asking Hubby ... '

He said, 'Well, not really, no. But thanks.'

A disapproving silence fell while she snipped away. And through our euphoria, Hubby and Mum were both struck with a vague sense of having failed their first test as the baby's parents ...

We are not all the same. There is not only one way for a father to celebrate his child's arrival in the world. And though it may be fashionable for men to park themselves 'at the business end' (and if there's a more coy expression in the English language I have yet to hear it) during the birth of their children – scissors and barbecue tools aloft in readiness for afterbirth severance and cooking – it doesn't mean it's necessarily what they or the baby's mother would prefer. Fashionable it may be, but it doesn't mean it's best.

And by the way, while we're on the subject, how can anyone seriously be expected to attach sentimental value to an afterbirth? Never mind the whole frying-it-with-garlic phenomenon (which I think we can all agree is cannibalistic and therefore a bit perverted), it's like attaching sentimental value to a turd. By the time either cord or afterbirth sees the light of day, it is human waste, nothing more – added to which it looks *completely disgusting*! Like a rejected prop from one of the *Alien* movies.

Pity the men though. In the birthing room. Neither nurse nor patient. Just something tactful and slightly pointless, trying not to feel queasy in between. It must be difficult for them sometimes, to know quite what to do with themselves.

Luckily (*quelle surprise!*), there's no shortage of places to look, should a Daddy-To-Be find himself in need of expert advice.

Here are the highlights from a ten-point 'perfect birth partner' checklist I just found from a popular baby website, BabyCentre.co.uk.

**\* Be aware of what she wants.**

*If she has a birth plan, make sure you bring it with you to hospital!*

**\* Be a one-person support team.**

*Do whatever she needs, from running to the cafeteria for a packet of sweets to getting her another drink.*

**\* Be prepared for surprises.**

*'I ended up rubbing my wife's foot all the way through labour,' says Chris.*

**\* Look after yourself!**

*The mum-to-be is the centre of attention, but you'll probably be spending the night at the hospital too, so don't forget to pack some things for yourself ... Pack a clean T-shirt ... Being able to change will help you feel fresher if you're up all night ... Comfortable shoes are essential.*

Okay dads? Shall we say it one more time? Comfortable shoes. Are essential.

Spare parts in soft-soled shoes. Poor sods. And no flowers afterwards. You've got to feel a tiny bit sorry for them.

## Writing A 'Birth Plan'

Always struck me as a harmless waste of time: a phony but well-intended system for lulling expectant mothers into imagining they have some kind of control over the process ahead. But I've since come to ask myself whether they may – unwittingly or otherwise – play a slightly more sinister role.

Consider this 'Conspiracy Theory A': it's possible Birth Plans are not simply pointless exercises for nervous, pregnant women, but part of a clever money-saving ruse on the part of our publicly funded hospitals. The NHS, as we all know, tries its level best to withhold epidurals from labouring mothers, which no matter how searing the agonies of the birthing process, will always be regarded as expensive and inessential.

So imagine if, in a moment of weakness, you wrote in your Birth Plan, along with the usual optimistic requests for scented candles and HypnoBirthing soundtrack CDs, that you want a natural birth, without painkillers, by the way (if you're bothering to write a birth plan at all), you're very likely to want this because it's what we are all encouraged to want and it sounds good and it sounds healthy and it sounds maternal … like you really, really love your unborn kid ☺. And above all, because it's impossible to imagine the pain of childbirth until you're in the throes of it.

But then the moment comes, and lo! Along with it the realisation (as it does for so many women) that the 'natural' option wasn't quite such a bright idea after all. You call for an epidural …

Your midwife might just hold up that idiotic bit of paper, written in a cosy sitting room months ago, when the threat of doctorly disapproval loomed far larger than the realities of such intense physical pain:

'Are you quite certain?' the midwife will ask you kindly, *as you begin to scream*. 'Are you sure you can't hold out a little longer? Because you said in your Birth Plan ... And we're doing so well! And we're so nearly there!'

... And by the time you have persuaded them that yes, you bloody well are certain, and no, you cannot hold out a little longer ... and they have promised you for the hundredth time that an 'anaesthetist is on the way' ... it will be too late.

There tends to be a lot of pressure to go for a natural birth, or a water birth, or a birth with minimal intervention ... and all sorts of reasons are offered, none of which makes any more sense to me than the Silent Birth option, beloved of Scientologists.

The point is, if a woman could actually imagine or fully remember the extraordinary drama and intense pain of childbirth, it might be worth her while to write down a plan to cope with it all. But since we can't, thankfully, or the human race would have died out long ago, it's simply another time-wasting mini-task for 'Mums-To-Be' which at best teeters on patronising.

I never wrote a 'Birth Plan'. Partly because I was too disorganised. For Baby Number 1, I certainly *meant* to; but I think, even then, I could sense it was likely to be a fruitless exercise. If I were to write one today (Haha! And thank goodness I don't need to!) ... this is what I would write:

Epidural, please.

Nice cuppa tea with two sugars, please.

Thank you.

Feel free to copy it out in your neatest, so you can give it to your midwife as and when.

**And good luck with that.**

# PART 3

# BABYCARE

*(And Some Possible Shortcuts)*

## Bonding

Business people, politicians, sociologists – they all invent words and procedures to lend their banal contributions to the national conversation an air of expertise. So it is with the process the baby experts call 'bonding'. Nevertheless, we must push through. You can't write a book about mummies and babies without talking about BONDING.

First of all: what is it exactly? I'm pretty certain it's what old-fashioned people call 'mother love'. Which love, of course, in real life, just sort of *happens* (for the vast majority of us) and does not preclude feelings of irritation, claustrophobia, or really quite acute boredom.

But that's too simple for the baby-advising brigade. It renders them and their patronising, faux-reassuring advice all but redundant. On the contrary, according to the website KidsHealth.org (and a million others like it): 'Bonding is a complex, personal experience that takes time. There's no magic formula and it can't be forced ...'

Thank you, choir.

New mummies are reassured that most of the ordinary tasks involved in the care of their new baby (*especially* breastfeeding, need I bother to mention?) are excellent 'tools' for 'bonding'. Which is a bit like saying lungs are an excellent tool for breathing. Nobody's arguing with it. But unless the lungs are, by some unfortunate accident, deficient, they don't need to be specifically and carefully introduced to a room full of air to know how to suck it in.

Needless to say, there is a font of advice out there explaining to Mumsie how best to breathe. I mean bond. Much of which seems to end with the faintly cute injunction not to worry. But why *would* a mother worry, unless it's been suggested to her that the process of loving her own adorable but sometimes irksome baby 'correctly' is in fact far more complicated than she realises; that it requires books, articles and innumerable websites to know how to do it properly, and that somehow or other she is almost certainly cocking it up? 'Bonding', we're told at MedicineNet.com, 'is a big, and sometimes scary word for new parents.'

Aww, *come on!*

Askamum.co.uk says bonding with baby is 'so important' they have provided a checklist of twenty ways to do it correctly, among them: 'blowing raspberries on a tiny tummy', 'regular morning snuggles under the duvet' and 'taking a babymoon' – which suggestion, frankly, is so inane I refuse to translate it for anyone … Okay, I will. It means, errrr – spending time with the baby.

The advice – and there is no shortage of it – seems to brook no middle ground. There is only one place to be when you're a loving and coping mother. (Luckily, with the right checklist anyone can get there!) And that is in the cloying, orgasmic land of Total Mummy Heaven.

'Begin by cradling your baby and gently stroking him or her in different patterns,' advises ivillage.co.uk. 'Smile.' (babycentre. co.uk) 'Look deep into your baby's eyes and watch how she stares back.' (babyzone.com) 'Lie him on the floor between your legs and just watch. You'll appreciate what an amazing thing you've created.' (askamum.co.uk) 'Smell your baby and let your baby smell you.' (ivillage.co.uk). 'Take a baby massage and/or baby yoga course.' (bondingwithbaby.co.uk) 'Play peekaboo' (emmasdiary.co.uk) 'Only *do* remember ... if you hide behind a cushion, you must appear again, preferably smiling ... '

## Bonding With Your Bump

There's many a slip 'twixt cup and lip ...' Or there isn't, actually, beyond a certain point in the pregnancy. But even so, it's hard not be a tiny bit superstitious. Bonding with an unborn child feels like a risky sort of a game: one that's quite hard to avoid, mind, in the later stages, when even the baby's limbs are discernible through the skin. Nevertheless, for fear of tempting fate, I tried quite hard to fight it. Against expert advice.

In any case, I don't think anyone really plays classical music to their bellies, do they? Or thinks beautiful thoughts for their unborn child's future peace of mind. It's just another fucking thing-to-do or *fail*-to-do, and feel vaguely inept for not attempting. All I do know is that of the three babies I brought into the world, the most easy-going, laid-back and cheerful was the one I carried when I was on the point of divorce. No beautiful thoughts. No classical music. More vicious fighting than during the rest of my life put together. Stuff that up your peace pipe, baby gurus. Studies show (or at any rate, mine do) that a bump is a bump, however beloved. And it cannot read your thoughts.

## Bonding With Daddy

I said I wouldn't patronise readers with meaningless studies. But I wanted to share this little peach, brought to us, in all its negativity and uselessness, by the energy company e.on:

*Babies who are bathed by their fathers at least three times a week are significantly less likely to experience difficulties making and keeping friends later on.*

Uber-parenting anxiety isn't only a mother's problem. Or it won't be for much longer. Looks like the experts are coming after Daddy too.

## Breast-Beating

Years ago, I went on a long road trip with a small group of friends. Our team leader (who owned the car) was an astonishingly lazy man with quite a bad drug problem – not that it's relevant. I dislike sitting in cars. But some people really love it. The lazy man with the drug problem was one such.

We drove for eight hours across the flat American landscape (with pit stops for him and his nozzer) until finally we reached our hotel. Instead of getting out of the car so we could check in, our team leader insisted on parking several blocks away, and then, with the engine still running, calling the hotel reception from his comfortable seat behind the wheel. I wanted to kill him – not that it's relevant. The moment brought with it a useful epiphany about the myriad ways we have each devised to satisfy our own particular forms of laziness. Some people love long car journeys. They love driving. It allows them to feel like they are *doing something*, even though they're not really; that is to say, they are not doing anything that requires more than the bare minimum of movement and thought, but they're doing just enough to prevent them from feeling they ought to be doing something else.

For years I had a similar approach to smoking. Just-having-a-cigarette is neither doing nothing nor is it doing something. It's a non-moment, invisibly suspended, somewhere between those two ghastly extremes. And now that I think about it, it's exactly that – the Time Out – that I miss most about having stopped.

For many, breastfeeding offers the same sort of relief. Fair enough. And why not? Having babies, let alone taking care of them, is exhausting. For people who don't have other things they might prefer to be doing, breastfeeding represents an excellent excuse to sit very still for ages – and I do mean *ages* – without anyone judging you for it, least of all – yourself.

And that's okay.

Or it's not okay.

What do I care? Who am I to say? Sit or don't sit. Breastfeed or don't breastfeed. I've done both. The sitting option can be remarkably relaxing and very cosy. But after a while, guess what? *It gets boring.*

Life is short. There is much to see and do. Spend too long on the sofa with your boob hanging out, drinking sugary tea and telling yourself breastfeeding aids weight loss (yeah, right) and the following things might happen.

Erm ...

Well, nothing.

And for a lot of women (not all), 'nothing' is not quite enough. Not when there's a perfectly decent alternative.

There's a new study every week, or so it seems. Non-breastfed children tend to be less good at javelin throwing, more inclined to adulterous thoughts in their sixth decade, less likely to be good at reading three-dimensional maps upside down ... There are studies, damn studies ... And above all, before everything sacred, there are statistics advocating the superiority of breast milk. But the fact is, babies thrive on bottled milk, and the evidence for this is so bountiful that it seems faintly idiotic even to have to point it out.

Nevertheless, given the virulence of the pro-breastfeeding brigade – the patronising bad mother Mini-Puckers that the non-breastfeeders are confronted with day in and day out – I'll say it once, just to be clear: bottle-fed babies tend to get fatter, faster, which I think we all agree is a good thing. They get fuller, faster, thereby freeing up time for their chief feeder to be more than a human milk machine. Also a good thing. Bottle-fed babies stay full for longer and therefore tend to sleep for longer. Bloody marvellous. Everybody's happier.

And yet, mysteriously, the Experts frown.

So frown back.

## Breastfeeding Children With Teeth And/Or Leather-Soled Shoes

'Go arn, go arn, go arrrrrn,' as Mrs Doyle would say. I couldn't put it better myself … *Any time, any place, anywhere.* Preferably live, on *Question Time,* with the other breast spurting milk around the studio in anticipation. That would be brave and also very funny. But know, too, that when you pull out that boob so defiantly, and shove it in the face of a child already able to stand beside your chair, it appears less like the Earth Mother than you may imagine, and more like a person with quite serious anger issues, careering boldy and defiantly off the rails. Which is fine … I suppose … Only please try to stay calm if everyone around starts giggling and retching at once.

## Breast Pump

Ah yes.

Don't even take it out of the box.

And by the way, if anyone's ever wondered why women find it quite hard to feel like sexual beings again after childbirth, look no further than this odious little contraption. I bought one for the first baby and used it, I think, three times before chucking it in the bin. It's unnecessary, mildly uncomfortable and – above all – it makes you look and feel completely ridiculous. Whoever invented it must have been a misogynist, sadist, weirdo, pervert ...

Or – unlikely but possible – just a nice, well-meaning cokehead. The only person I ever found with anything to say in the contraption's favour tells me that her breast pump was invaluable after all-night drink'n'drug benders. The following day she would always take care to express the milk that might contain residues of the previous night's excesses and throw it away, and then continue to breastfeed as normal, the day after ...

*Pop, chop, pump and chuck* ... she called it. And by the way, her children, weaned long since, are clever and kind, healthy and beautiful – and thriving.

Maybe Tommee Tippee might consider using it as a slogan?

## Babies At Night

Can be a nuisance. Mothers of newborns sometimes find it hard to think or speak about anything else ... Which, let's face it, is often a good reason to avoid them. Poor things.

*I generally put him down at 7, but then at 10 he tends to have a full nappy, so I try to wake him and sort of squeeze in another feed and then hope against hope. He slept through til 4 last Friday – which was fabulous ... but normally he begins to whimper around*

*3 ... If I'm lucky, I can get him back to sleep again and he'll go through to 6 ... I'm trying to get him into a routine but then I hear him sobbing his little eyes out and I can't just leave him, I CAN'T DO IT. <u>He's</u> wailing. <u>I'm</u> awake ... and I'm knackered. I don't think I've ever been so knackered in my life ...*

Aye.

Vast fortunes have been made advising women on what to do and what not to do to get babies to sleep through the night. Every baby expert has a theory. It's something they seem to feel very, very strongly about, often promoting polar opposite opinions and techniques. I dare say all the techniques work eventually, since humans past babydom generally tend to sleep during the night.

The one thing that all the experts seem to agree on, however, is that it's a rotten idea to do the one thing which actually works, and which most mothers most instinctively long to do; namely to plonk the baby in bed beside you and let it suckle. The baby goes quiet. Both parties conk out again at once. And it's lovely, actually. Better than lovely – really quite close to perfection. Peaceful, friendly, private, cosy and loving.

Experts talk of cot death and our hearts stop still. They talk about mothers rolling over on top of their babies and accidentally suffocating them, but unless a mother is truly, madly and excessively inebriated and perhaps grotesquely fat, we all know in our hearts that it could never happen. For the same reason we don't roll over and fall out of bed every night.

Actually. Only more so. And for the same reason that mothers wake up at the first sound of their baby's whimper, (while a father can sleep obliviously through it, or at least pretend to.) There is an instinct to protect our babies that runs far deeper than mere sleep, and which makes a nonsense of the gurus' counter-intuitive and stubbornly joyless precautions. Defy them if you dare. I did.

## Leaving Babies To Cry

People have amazingly strong opinions on this one, too. Especially the older generation, whose 'leave them to cry' approach (and I shall return to the matter of where to put disposable nappies shortly: it's the other thing which sends the oldies crazy with irritation) sometimes, I think, carries a tiny hint of sadism.

'They need to learn,' the Oldies cry. (*Learn what exactly, I always wondered?*) Babies cry.

'If you keep picking them up they'll never learn ... *We* were left to cry. It didn't do us any harm ...'

There's no proof of that of course. We might all have turned out completely different and much, much better if we had never been left to cry.

Too bad. Too late.

The point is, there are systems, inflexible and diametrically opposed, whose proponents – as with the sleep training – are equally adamant about their rightness. Among the most noisome, currently, are Claire Verity of 'no eye contact at bed time' fame, keen on leaving babies to cry indefinitely; Gina Ford of 'Contented Baby' fame, keen on 'controlled crying' … (as if 'controlled crying' were any different from 'crying'). Both involve leaving a baby to cry. But add 'controlled' and it lends the same *lack of action* a sort of selfless respectability, which guilt-ridden modern mothers so crave. And of course there is 'Dr Bill' (Dr William Sears), famous for his unfeasibly inconvenient 'babywearing-attachment' theory.

None of the three, I can't help mentioning, has borne babies of their own.

In any case, they're all bonkers, frankly. *In my opinion.* (Can I say that, without getting sued?) Sometimes it's horrible leaving your baby to cry. Sometimes it's horrible not to.

And no matter in what state of 'horrible' we find ourselves, the sound of our own baby's cry is, to most mothers, a specific and acute form of torture. My only piece of advice is this: when a mother finds herself in the latter state of horrible, i.e., unable to be in the same room with the baby for a moment longer, be sure to close any doors between the two of you. Put yourself out of earshot. Switch off the baby alarm. And if its lights continue to flash, throw the bloody thing in the bin. Give it to some other mother to torment herself with! You probably never should have bought the stupid machine in the first place.


## Disposable Nappies

Herewith: a salute for the women who recycle their terry cloths, who painstakingly pack them up into reusable buckets and send them off in vans to be sterilised – or whatever it is they do. Their saintliness leaves me reeling.

Everybody knows disposable nappies are not environment-ally friendly. Then again, nor is having a baby. Nor is anything, really. When you get down to it ... And there are some things I will do for the planet, and other things which, since I'm bloody well living on it, I feel the planet must do for me. Finding a home for my offspring's dirty nappies has always fitted into the second category. That's all I have to say about that.

The in-my-day, *never-harmed-me*, leave-them-to-cry, yellow-toothed battleaxe brigade tend to get quite uppity about disposables. As previously mentioned. They complain about the way young mothers put nappies in the household rubbish (although nappies tend to be wrapped in sweet-smelling nappy bags that are often far more hygienic and less stinky than other things chucked into a household bin). Clever battleaxes strengthen their anti-disposable arguments by focusing their ire on the environmental impact.

But we all know it's jealousy *really*.

Never mind the Pill. Never mind power steering, equal pay, maternity leave ... never mind the Internet! The greatest leap forward in modern times – for mothers at least – has to be the Disposable Nappy.

I salute the Terry Cloth Angels. I suppose. But with some bemusement. Life is quite chore-laden enough for mothers of nappy-aged children. I would suggest that such time-consuming and inconvenient attempts at saving the planet might be reserved for a less fraught stage in a mother's own life, and achieved via a less repellent method.

## *Injections, Health Visitors And Baby Clinics*

Ask health visitors a specific question about your baby or about babycare in general and they never seem to have much of an answer. Also – which is more confusing – they tend to remain implacably untroubled by their almost unerring inability to help. They pull friendly faces, call your baby 'Baby' and you 'Mum'.

And, no matter what, no matter how reassuringly they present themselves, there is always a sense that they are spies: checking up on your fitness as a mother, looking out for reasons to report you and 'Baby' to a higher authority. I may be repeating myself, but I don't need a graph to see if my baby is chubby enough. I don't need a mysteriously unhelpful spy-nurse, calling me 'Mum', clucking with disapproval when I tell her I'm not breastfeeding and making my baby cry by putting its little naked body on a weighing machine ... I don't need these things. I don't need the State to fill in a line chart to be reassured that my baby is thriving. I don't need unknown women asking me, *sans* eye contact, as my shivering baby screams on their unnecessary weighing machines, 'And how's mummy coping?'

Mummy is coping as well as can be expected. Thanks very much.

The State isn't all bad ... And I thank them for all injections, and – most assuredly – for the well-intentioned kindness many of them do offer. And for the kindness they no doubt offer to those who are in genuine need. But the universal, regular weigh-ins? Unpleasant and undignified for the baby; tiresome and undermining for their mother.

I never could get to the bottom of whether they were obligatory. Certainly, in the early years, with the first baby, there was a sense that they may have been. In any case, as I discovered, whether you bother to attend is up to you. Thankfully, nobody chases you up. Or they didn't me. I can't – ahem, for the moment – exactly lay my hands on the infamous Little Red Book to verify this, but I'm not sure that I attended any weigh-ins at all for Baby Number 3. I had a lot of work on – and other children. There simply wasn't the time (let alone the inclination) to hang about for unspecified periods in germ-soaked surgery waiting rooms. And Baby Number 3 always looked well. A sort of normal size for a baby. Nice and fat and cheerful, because of all that formula milk. There didn't seem to be any point.

## Bedtime, Routines And Early Starts

Baby Number 1 was subjected to a preposterous 'routine': eating and sleeping were monitored and managed to the ounce and the minute. It was remarkably unrelaxing and it didn't last long. Baby Number 2 survived through a muddle of half-hearted routine and drunken confusion, due to my father dying shortly after he was born. Baby Number 3 slept and ate whenever she felt like it.

Fast-forward to today. Baby Number 3 is six years old.

During the school week, she sometimes has to be cajoled into hitting the sack, but during weekends and holidays, like her older siblings, she goes to bed more or less (not entirely) when she likes, and has done for several years now. Sometimes – quite often, actually – she conks out on the sofa with the rest of us, and sometimes she says, 'I'm tired, please take me to bed.' So I do that. It seems to be okay. She has boundless energy. And because she goes to bed at a civilised hour, she wakes at a reasonably civilised hour, too; allowing her parents to sleep during those precious weekend early mornings.

The older ones learned early on how to amuse themselves at antisocial hours of the morning. They learned how to switch on the telly, and how to fetch themselves a bowl of cereal while their parents slumbered.

This harmless and mutually satisfactory system (the children got to watch all sorts of drivel without being interrupted) sometimes used to be a source of friction, however, when staying in the company of other parents, who were more fussy or assiduous than we were. Their children, having been sent to bed earlier, would inevitably run out of sleep earlier, too. At which point the children would, understandably, insist on getting out of bed, and then – less understandably – expect full-throttle clown-and-waiter service from their exhausted parents from that moment on.

I don't know why the parents didn't simply chuck their children the remote control. But they didn't ... And it wouldn't have mattered either way (or not to me), except that, if our children also happened to be up or (more likely) were woken by the early risers, then they too would then be welcomed into the pre-dawn play club.

Conscientious, pasty, sulky, and *so tired* in their nightwear, the parents would cajole our children into eating appropriate levels of Coco Pops, offer them boiled eggs and freshly squeezed Anywayup Cups of organic apple juice ... and fuss over them

and *fuss*

and *fuss*

and *fuss* ...

My children, though bemused by this intense attention, wouldn't object to it. If somebody *wanted* to offer them fried eggs and chocolate drink, and do colouring and plasticine and jigsaw puzzles with them at 6 o'clock in the morning, who were they to argue? Why not?

Why not indeed?

The barbed remarks would come thick and fast when we two parents finally joined the breakfast party. (For barbed remarks are the feature of every early-rising kiddie Coco Pop provider.) A stream of unsolicited bulletins – about what each of our children had eaten or not eaten for breakfast, how quickly they had been persuaded to put on their dressing gowns ... drink their juice ... AND WHAT OF IT? I longed to cry. We didn't ask for your cloying uber-care. We didn't want it. My children are *better off* learning to look after themselves. You should've just left them to their own devices and gone back to bed. They would have been fine without you ...

Is it time for a Bloody Mary yet?

## Bedtime And Alcohol

I read an article at the weekend which asked readers to ask themselves if they were 'parentoholics'. They were invited to fill in a questionnaire.

Another day, another new thing for Parents to worry about, then.

Q: What's a parentoholic?
A: It's someone who looks forward to having a glass of wine the moment they put their children to bed!

Actually, on closer examination, it's someone who looks forward to having a glass of wine the moment they put their children to bed, *and then* ... drinks like a mad fish, fucks up their life as a result and in all respects behaves like a common-or-garden alcoholic. Ho hum. Being an alcoholic is clearly a problem. What annoys me is that it should ever have been so impertinently juxtaposed with Being A Parent – who drinks as soon as the children are in bed. What the hell's wrong with that?

My only beef with it is that we should be expected to wait that long. Do I have a glass of wine as soon as I put the children to bed? Good God, I have one long before! As soon as I close down the computer. Why? Because I feel like it. Alcohol, for most of us, has a pleasant effect on mood. Yeah. That's probably a reason why it's so popular. It makes us merrier. And I don't

125

really understand why this is something we feel we should hide from our children. In my experience, children rather prefer it when their parents are merry and relaxed. As indeed (need I add?) do the parents.

Am I a parentoholic? Hard to tell. I drink every day, and with pleasure. Which I think puts a hefty tick in the YES box. On the other hand, I drink long before the children go to bed, which means I don't helter-skelter towards the bottle like a mad thing, the moment they're out of sight. Which I think means a tick in the NO box. Or maybe not. Who cares? In any case, if I waited until they were all in bed, I might easily die of thirst.

Being an idle mother, keen on relaxing, and one who avoids all chores wherever possible, it tends not to be that taxing having the children around. (*Of course* you can reach it, darling! Don't be wet. There's bound to be a ladder somewhere ...) Quite the opposite in fact. Which is probably why I rarely insist on them going to bed. In fact, so long as they're not squabbling or creating unnecessary tasks for me, there are no people in the world I feel happier to hang out with.

If you refuse to be a slave to your children, resist the temptation to fuss over them, or to issue them endlessly with non-crucial guidelines and instructions ... and if you insist that they repay such thoughtfulness by not issuing *you* with non-crucial chores ... If we could all simply *let each other be* ... then there wouldn't be such a parental sense of being 'on duty' when the children are up and about, and parents wouldn't feel like they were 'off duty' when the children finally went to bed.

And the frantic 'parentoholic' rush to hit the bottle, come the end of the day, is reduced to altogether more seemly levels of gentle enthusiasm. Amen.

NB: Obviously, with children under two and a half years old, this system doesn't work so well. At this early stage, when children are still so helpless and foolish they can't even carry their own ladders, it's impossible to relax much while they're still up; and impossible not to feel relieved when they finally go to bed. Not to worry! Though it's hard to imagine at the time, *this phase of family life will pass*. A few years of more full-throttle parentoholicism may be unavoidable – until children are old enough to take themselves to the lavatory, pour themselves a glass of water, go upstairs and put their own pyjamas on. At which point, evening drinking can be approached with a little more moderation and elegance, once again.

# PART 4

# CHILDCARE

*(Because Minimum-effort Parenting Saves YOU
Time And Money. And It's Fun For All The Family!)*

## Unparenting

It's annoying, isn't it, when you think you've had an original idea and then it turns out someone else has already come up with it. It happened to me as a child when I came up with 'I think therefore I am'. Dammit. Even if nobody believes me. I now discover, in the form of an exciting and fast-growing new parenting movement called 'Unparenting', that something similar has happened once again. Unparenting, as you might discern from its name, promotes a hands-off approach to child-rearing: non-prescriptive, engaged, affectionate, fluid, open-minded, adaptable, liberal, mutually respectful: to which admirable mix I would only inject a defiant shot of feminism. And suggest *mutually gratifying*. It's a modern truism, as discussed, that motherhood should be a one-way street, a no-right-of-way relationship structured for the kiddie-widdies' benefit and for the kiddie-widdies benefit alone. But it's unrealistic. It's silly, sentimental, anti-female, and creepy.

On a more positive note, although galling to learn I am just another voice in a growing movement, it is exhilarating to discover that I'm not, after all, on my own out here, crying for freedom and common sense into the playground. If others are

131

coming to the same – or similar – conclusions, there is hope for the future yet.


## Shared Parenting

Poor old Nick Clegg was getting a hammering on the radio this morning. He was trying to flag a new government initiative that would allow mothers and fathers equal share of what used to be called 'maternity leave'. He explained what good sense it made, now that women are the chief breadwinners in many households. He seemed to think it was a rotten shame that so many women had to sacrifice their careers to stay home with their babies, while so many fathers – who would be more than happy to stay home with their babie – are forced to go out and win bread.

Which is all very well, in theory. Nick Clegg should be congratulated, at least for trying. And there's nothing wrong with his suggestions exactly, except that they're not really very helpful. It seems to me, with the best will in the world, he's got hold of the wrong end of the stick.

He talked about the heartbreak suffered by men who long to be at home with their children. But the truth is – in general men don't suffer *much* heartbreak. *In general*, even the most loving of fathers (Nick included I dare say, no matter how many snippets he feeds us about making it home in time for kiddie bathtime) find it a simple thing to leave the breakfast table and walk out of the door. They don't beat themselves up about not being there for their children in the way that so many mothers do. And maybe it's cultural. (There are exciting experiments related to enforced paternity leave ongoing in magnificent Scandinavia – and perhaps we shall even discover that the intensity of mother love is all in our conditioning after all.) But in the meantime – maybe we just do we love our children more.

From the moment our babies come into the world, mothers are more alert to their cries, more intricately and intensely concerned for their every comfort. For the time being at least, it's just the way it mostly is. For better or worse. And Nick Clegg, with all the goodwill in the world, can legislate until he's blue in the face about how it *ought* to be in a modern, civilised, equal world, but it doesn't alter the fact that mothers, in general, tend to find it far harder than fathers to be separated from their young.

I get heartache if I am to spend a night away from mine. I get heartache *several days in advance of the separation*. In fact – it probably sounds wet, but it's hardly unusual – I get (slight) heartache if I know in the morning that I won't make it home in time to see them before they go to bed. Mother love is an affliction (or sometimes it feels that way) that fades, I sincerely hope, when the children grow up and leave the nest. It's an affliction that rarely (ever?) hits fathers to quite the same degree.

I don't want to surrender my role as first-port-of-call parent. Absolutely not! I never want to share my role as mother. I love my role as mother! I only want to avoid making it any more wearisome, costly or complicated than it needs to be.

If Mr Clegg, with his sympathetic-to-mothers hat on, could legislate against – I don't know: pointless after-school activities that entail chauffeuring, organising playdates more than a couple of days in advance, complicated costume requirements for school shows and assemblies, unnecessary simpering at the school gate ... or, shucks, maternal guilt, he might actually be on to something.

## Wet Dads

How is it that some people – the British in particular, perhaps? – having procreated with (arguably) some degree of success, feel they no longer have even the faintest duty to remain if not alluring then at least not repugnant to the other sex? I ask the question about women, so many of whom seem to surrender their sexuality at the altar of mummydom.

But at least with women you can understand how it comes about. The process of pregnancy and birth, breaking waters, leaking boobs and torn vaginas, not to mention breastfeeding, sick-wiping, etc., etc., ... can bend the old self-image out of shape. Just a tad. Feeling like a sexual being again after all that takes, for most of us, time, sleep, and also a concerted effort. But the men? The Wet Dad Brigade, soft-voiced and squeaky-soled, who seem to grow bosoms as their partner's baby bump develops, who sit on the floor in communal antenatal classes, empathising their way through the pelvic floor exercises ...

What's their excuse? *What happened to them?* Were they like that at school? Was this the face they wore when they were courting the future mothers of their children? Or did they just gulp back too much oestrogen in the tap water in the intervening period?

It begs the question (or it does to me): how did they ever get laid in the first place?

You see them everywhere: the Wet Dad Brigade – at parental get-togethers and wandering the aisles of supermarkets and, occasionally, even married to friends. They talk to their children in special voices, often (which isn't simply irritating, it's gross) referring to themselves in the third person: 'Daddy wants you to sit at the table and eat your carrot pap. What did Daddy tell you earlier? Daddy's getting a teeny bit cross now ... .'

I like to imagine Daddy much later, when the other adults have gone and the kiddies are safely tucked up in bed, and Daddy's not a teeny bit cross any more. He is on his tod, soft-soled sandals warming by the natural gas fire, relaxing at last in the safe early evening. ... While mummy's upstairs, rubbing soothing gels into her well-worn nipples, feeling slightly smug, perhaps, about the broken husk of a man she shares her bed with every night, Wettie Hubby is downstairs in the sitting room, jacking off feverishly to online porn ... possibly involving fluffy, dead animals. I sort of hope he is. For everyone's sake, really. But mostly for my own peace of mind. Somebody's got to be watching that stuff, after all. Let's imagine it's him.

## Stay-At-Home Dads/House Husbands

Are not the same as Wet Dads. In fact, I think it takes a certain amount of courage, on the part of both parents, to travel along this still quite unconventional pathway. At my children's schools and nurseries, there have always been at least a couple of house husbands on duty – more, I note, since the recession. Some are only passing through, between redundancies. Others are there for the duration. In either case, they tend to cut rather solitary figures.

The bottom rung (i.e., super-thick) stay-at-home mother brigade find them disconcerting, I think, and treat them with slight disdain. I am not sure why this is. Perhaps they feel their turf is being threatened; that their roles as financially dependent Wives And Mothers are being somehow undermined by such a grotesque perversion of the natural order? Who knows what it is about house husbands that rubs them up so, but something clearly does.

## Fathers And Daughters

The only time I feel a real surge of old-fashioned feminist dislike for the other sex is when I hear them talk with coy, facetious horror about the prospect of their young daughters one day forming relationships with men. It's a convention, isn't it, even for the Wet Dad Brigade, to make cutesy He-Man noises of protest about the future sexual relations of their precious little girls. 'No man will be good enough!' they declare. 'I swear – no man's ever going near her.' *Chuckle, chuckle,* go the dinner guests. *'How sweet!'*

It's meant to convey, in deprecating and humorous fashion, the immeasurable love and esteem a father has for his little girl. And perhaps it does convey that. But if so, what does it convey about the love and esteem he has for all the other women in his life? His wife, for example? The He-Man declarations take as understood that no loving father would wish upon his daughter what he himself has wished upon all the women he ever loved and desired. And there's nothing terribly sweet about that. Sounds psychopathic to me.

And worryingly conceited, too, since they pivot on the assumption that in heterosexual relationships all men exploit all women and that women, no matter what, will always emerge the losers.

Dream on, gents.


## Boundaries

Every child needs boundaries, so the wisdom goes. It's something grown-up mummies and daddies say to each other over their cocktail sausages at nursery school parents' evenings, when they're still a little fresh to the We Are Parents protocols and they've run out of conversation about the weather. But I've always thought it sounded, at best, deluded – like a grown-up practising their grown-upness: at worst, sinister; hinting of the wilful stupidity of lazy bureaucrats and of a dangerous penchant for absolute power.

Every Child Needs Boundaries. What does it mean in any case? What 'boundaries' are mummies and daddies referring to? Are they really suggesting, over their cocktail sausages, that children should have their limits laid down for them in advance, and that they must be made to understand, absolutely, that these limits are non-negotiable?

Do not watch telly on weekdays – *but what if there's something really good on?*
Do not answer back – *but what if there is still a point to be made?*
Do not eat sandwiches in the bath – *but shucks, what if nobody leaves any crumbs?*

It's nonsense. Has to be. After all, there is almost nothing in the run of ordinary adult life that isn't negotiable; almost no boundary that isn't at least a little nudgeable. And the more educated a person is, the more confident and successful, the richer, cleverer and more attractive they are, the better they damn well know it. Why would we not want to let our children in on this important truth?

Aside from the fact that 'boundaries' are often tiresome to uphold (and sometimes patently absurd, quite rightly rendering the 'boundary enforcer' a figure of mockery and derision), boundaries serve almost no purpose. Not to the child and not to the parent. Every situation is different. Every interaction is different. Every individual is different. Every conflict is annoying in a different way. No one involved is a robot. And nor, boys and girls, are Mums and Dads always right!

In fact, in any given child–parent conflict, Mums and Dads – tired, impatient, misguided, ignorant of the facts, or just too old, deaf, narrow-minded and stupid to understand them, are probably in the *wrong* no more or less often than their child is. At which point, perhaps we might be better off allowing ourselves a little room for manoeuvre, if only to save face. Why go to the inconvenience of lumbering ourselves with an inflexible system, which insists, above all and no matter what, that we are right and our word is final, when half the time it's reasonably likely not to be the case? It's like pretending we don't fart.

Our children will find out sooner or later what nincompoops and plonkers their loving parents really are. They will discover what fools and flops and flakes – and lovable farters – make up the adult world in which they must one day learn to survive. The sooner we climb down from our self-erected pedestals and treat them, and ourselves, not as pre-defined Persons in pre-designated Roles, but as free and flawed individuals, *allies* in a lonely and confusing universe, the happier and easier it might be for everyone.

I have only two requirements of my children (aside from the one, long-established, to make eye contact when saying thank you to waiters). Firstly, that, in exchange for the roof above their heads and the chocolate biscuits in the cupboard; in exchange for all the emotional and financial investment, the boundless love and care, and for all the devotion, thought and unconditional support that has been put into their free and independent futures ... that they invest something into their futures themselves, think for themselves and embrace the world around them with energy.

And secondly and obviously: not to be cruel.

Are they 'boundaries'? Maybe they are. Beyond those, the only real boundary depends on my boredom threshold on the day. This, in turn, depends on the colour and height of the sky, whether I've just been fired or been offered a pay rise, whether or not I have a hangover – and finally, whether or not a child has done what it's done, taken what it's took, with sufficient intelligence and charm ... that they can somehow find a way to wriggle out of it. Because, of course, if they're smart about it, don't make too much noise, don't cause too much bother, and, above all, if they don't get caught ... he or she can get away with pretty much anything.

Welcome to the world.


## A Mother Is Not A Friend

A favourite assertion made by the grown-ups and the experts in their relentless mission to quash our spontaneity and joy ...

But of course a mother is a friend.

After all, what is a friend?

Somebody you love and trust (and vice versa); somebody whose mistakes you forgive and whose successes you rejoice in (and vice versa); whom you respect and who respects you; someone who makes you laugh and makes you reconsider (and vice versa); with whom you have many things in common, whom you care about and who cares about you, whom you interest and who interests you, and for whom you are willing to fight ...

I honestly don't know which of the above isn't also to be hoped for (mutually) in a relationship between a mother and her children.

It doesn't mean you have to sit around getting high together. That would be awkward ... Or at any rate, I would find it uncomfortable. It doesn't mean all sorts of things: that your children are the best audience for a frank conversation about the possible limitations and irritations of their beloved father, the agonising pointlessness of existence, or the fact that you or he (or both) have just taken a lover. *Duh*. But of course it's a friendship! My children are my friends. Most certainly. And I am their friend – their close and loyal friend – and I sincerely hope I always will be.


## Mother's Day

My mother decreed that it was soppy, sentimental nonsense, mercilessly exploited – possibly even invented – by greedy purveyors of expensive soaps and decent chocolates. So we were never encouraged to celebrate Mother's Day as children.

Clearly, that was a mistake. It should be milked for all it's worth.

## Father's Day

Soppy, sentimental nonsense, mercilessly exploited – possibly even invented – by greedy purveyors of useless sporting accessories and hilarious toilet books. I don't think we can get away with ignoring it altogether without risking a reduction of services in the reciprocal event. Nevertheless, a child's hand-drawn card or something similar, ought, I feel, to be more than enough.

## Feeding Children

It all begins with the Lactation Nazis, as my friend from the Big Apple calls them. The kindly health advisers who tell us there is only one right way to feed our babies, and that everything else, though it does the job, will only ever be second best. Since only a tiny minority of women manage to stick with the recommended one hundred per cent breastfeeding approach for very long, most mothers launch themselves into the maze of toddler and child-feeding with an already quite familiar sense of guilt and failure hanging over them.

So. I seem to remember that the dogma regarding when to start feeding a baby solids changed in the interval between one or other of my babies. God knows what advice they're giving to mothers this week, but we can be sure as hell they'll be delivering it with the same dogmatic certainty they delivered the other advice the week before.

In the meantime, it seems to be reasonably obvious that you start feeding a baby solids when it has drunk all its milk and still appears to be hungry.

But anyway ...

A word on Cooking For Baby.

The Beaba Babycook Duo Steamer-Blender, available for you (at time of writing) for just £169.95 at the nation's favourite shop, 'steams, blends, defrosts and reheats' your baby's dindins. Added to which, apparently, it's 'easy to clean', and it 'preserves vitamins'!

Point Number One: What's wrong with an Adultcook – also known as 'an oven'. Most kitchens already have one.

Point Number Two: Errr. What's wrong with the shop-bought jars? Embellished and enhanced, when feeling especially energetic, by the occasional genuine article, squished-up banana?

I used to watch my girlfriends – ragged with exhaustion already – batch-steaming bits of broccoli and carrot, mushing them up and putting them into ice-cube trays for the freezer. I am not a nutritionist, but *everyone knows* food reheated from frozen loses vitamins and taste. (Not that babies have much in the way of taste buds anyway.) So what's the point of it? Why bother?

I did it for a month or so with Baby Number 1, only because everyone else was doing it: shoved a fucking broccoli stalk in and out of a series of small receptacles and into the freezer, to clog up space. It meant we had no ice-cubes, because no one ever remembered to buy an extra ice-cube tray. It also meant extra mess, added chores and boredom, and time spent fussing with saucepans that could have been spent relaxing in front of the telly. Or learning Portuguese. So I bought some jars, amused myself mildly, choosing from the truly vast array of flavours available, and never looked back. The baby didn't appear to enjoy the hand-mushed broccoli any more or any less than the jarred stuff, and didn't consume any more or less of it, either. I got to watch a tiny bit more telly/learn a bit more Portuguese. And, above all, of course, the baby continued to grow and thrive. *Todos ganha,* as I understand they say in Lisbon. *Criança feliz, feliz mãe.*

For sure, factory-made jars of baby food may work out more expensive than the home-cooked variety. (If you don't count the cost of time spent mushing your own broccoli, which could have been spent shorting the market/writing bestsellers/ taking in the neighbours' washing. Also, of course, assuming nobody's invested in a Beaba Babycook Duo Steamer-Blender @ £169.95.) The cost-saving aspect of home-cooked baby pap is often emphasised by the carey-sharey baby advisers. And I am all for saving money where I can, when it's practical – but, but, *but* – we're talking *pennies*, here. Babies eat virtually nothing in any case. Given the phenomenal cost of bringing children into the world, feeding them, clothing, entertaining and educating them, the money saved by hand-steaming your own carrots is laughable.

To the experts and the Mumgelicals who prefer to scowl at the jar feeders, while smiling nonsensically at their tiny saucepans, I say this:

Steam and mush away, if you want to: sometimes it's fun to mix and stir. Especially when hubby's out at the golf club again, for example, and *não existe absolutamente nada na televisão*. But you're making life harder than you need to.

I recommend the Heinz Cheesy Tomato Pasta Stars: £6 for ten jars at asda.com, as I write. Just pop in the microwave, Mum (only do take care!), and switch that telly back on!


## Healthy Snax

It's hard enough getting from A to B with a toddler at the best of times, bearing in mind how slowly they walk, how little they understand the concept of time or of deadlines, or of the word 'hurry', or the importance of remembering where they left their shoes. In the winter, there's likely to be an added fifteen minutes' preparation time before leaving the house, helping them on with coats, gloves and hats ... And then, depending on the duration and distance of the journey ahead, there will be *luggage*. Truck Loads of the stuff: nappies and baby wipes and plastic toys and dummies and pushchairs and rain covers and high chairs and sun hats and sun blocks and car seats and travel cots and teddy bears and nappy bags and muslin cloths – in fact just thinking about it makes me want to weep with gratitude and joy that my children have outgrown that phase of their development.

Why then would any mother want to add to these – sometimes seemingly insurmountable obstacles – by making the process of *getting out of the house* any more difficult than it already is? And yet ...

What is it with those little Tupperware snack boxes? It's as if children under three years old can't travel to the bus stop or walk across their own bloody sitting room without a hygienically packaged healthy snackette, if not already in their gob, at least within immediate reach of it.

You see them everywhere: in other people's cars and other people's kitchens, in other people's handbags and wedged between the handlebars of other people's pushchairs. Eezi-open, eezi-cleen, toddler-safe, airtight, snap-shut, germ-free, teeny-tiny plastic tubs, filled with pre-cut carrot bits. Little slices of apple. Miniature breadsticks ... And I am bewildered.

A toddler's snack in a toddler snack box is simply one more thing to prepare, carry, clean, leave behind on public transport, gather dust in the back seat of a car, or rot at the bottom of a handbag ... It's one more thing for a child to whinge about. And it's completely unnecessary.

Children aren't like sheep and horses (and possibly elephants?). They don't need to graze all day long.

## Juice

See above. 'Juice' is good for treats. But for every day it strikes me as somewhat excessive. It's an extra cost, an extra weight in a shopping basket, an extra space in a cupboard, an extra product to run out of, an extra thing to prepare in the general rigmarole of feeding children. It's fattening, tooth-rotting and actually (as with the constant-need-for-healthy-snack-in-gob scenario above) there's something vaguely effete about small children whingeing for 'juice' with their dindins, which makes me want to prod them sharply (when the parents aren't looking) and whisper a single word: SPOILT.

What's wrong with tap water?

## Fussy Eating

Remember the olden days, when the adults still had hang-ups about 'rationing'? They used to whip themselves into frenzies of puritanical irritation when confronted by their children's delicate palates and fussy eating habits. It was a *thing* – a bit like the London Olympics last summer – which united every adult, apparently. No matter what colour, creed or background, children had to be made to clean their plates.

Most of us have been at the receiving end of the older generation's clean-plate fetish at some point, I'm sure. I know I have. At home, with my gourmand family, over Jerusalem artichoke and lovage soups and *Suleiman's Pilaf* and ... never mind. At school, alone in the dining hall after everyone had left, gagging and weeping over tapioca, banana custard, tepid semolina with dried skin on top. The background strum was just the same: *'Waste not, want not/think of the starving Africans/ you don't know how lucky you are.'* The thought of lovage soup, by the way, still makes my stomach heave.

Anyway, it's probably because so many in my generation endured similar scenes in their childhood that we tend to be so gentle with, not to say indulgent of, our own children's nutritional peccadilloes. I don't know anyone who forces their children to finish food they actively dislike any more. I certainly don't.

On the other hand, I don't offer them a 'menu choice', either. It's troublesome enough preparing one 'meal option', for heaven's sake, let alone an array of them. So they can eat what's on offer, or not eat it. If they don't eat it they'll probably be hungry. And they will make up for it later. Or maybe they can fill up on bread, which is nice and cheap. Or not. It doesn't really matter and I don't really care. They certainly aren't going to starve.

## Organic Food

Is a waste of money. Studieshaveshown. Or some studies-haveshown. Enough of them, anyway, to persuade me not to bother.

A bit like novels with 'Shortlisted for the Booker' on the cover. If a food has 'organic' on the label, I take care to leave it on the shelf.

## Allergies, Intolerances And Other Health Alerts

One of my children is slightly allergic to peaches. Her lips swell up and her throat itches. Or rather, that's what used to happen. I eventually took her to the doctor, who did a test and informed us that she was also allergic to hazelnuts, which she wasn't really. And after that, I don't know quite what happened … Peaches aren't something that feature too large in an ordinary northern European's diet. The impetus to resolve the 'problem' sort of faded away.

We were meant to see another consultant who would tell us what else she was allergic to, but we never quite got round to it. I said, 'Maybe you shouldn't eat peaches. Or hazelnuts.' Which suggestions she chose to ignore. Now the peach allergy has gone, and the hazelnut allergy continues to travel incognito, if it travels at all. And everything seems to be okay. The end.

Cracking story, eh? (There's nothing quite like an unsolicited food-intolerance update to get the old heart beating.) A woman I met at dinner last week had a son who couldn't eat gluten. When shopping she had to be ever so careful, she told me, about identifying each and every ingredient on the label – zzzzzzzzzzzzzzzzz.

Anyway. Some allergies are all too real. Clearly. (With a nod to my fine godson.) But you can't help wondering whether some may possibly be a teeny tiny bit more real than others? Keep yer pants on! I'm just saying, once you venture down the ask-a-consultant-why-my-kid's-a-bit-whiny route, it can be quite hard to turn back. The initial, 'he has a tummy ache when he eats stuff that's chewy' ... may soon turn into an obstacle course, riddled with unnecessary challenges: weeks and months spent tussling with NHS appointments personnel, followed, eventually, by lists of previously unsuspected problems and disorders – and of hazelnuts better avoided. Children grow out of a lot of allergies naturally; and if there's anything better to avoid in life – all walks of life – it's lists of things better avoided.

I'm also saying ... that I can't help *noticing* ... that the more neurotic, underemployed and middle-class the mothers, the higher the incidence of -apses, -ipses, -opses and -ergies in their sometimes slightly whiny offspring.

But listen. What do I know? Perhaps that's just a coincidence.

## *Sniffles And Sickly Children*

After many years working for small, struggling private companies, a friend of mine took a job in the public sector. It turned out to be a pleasant job and she was reasonably happy. But it required quite a period of adjustment. There was, she said, a fundamental – actually quite a shocking – difference in her new colleagues' approach to work: most noticeably in how healthy they believed they needed to feel before they might be willing to get down to it.

On a Wednesday morning, soon after she had started the job, she received an email from a senior colleague who had decided not to come in for the rest of the week. The reason given was:

*'I'm not feeling one hundred per cent. Not even eighty per cent actually and I don't want to spread anything around. At this point I think it's better for me to stay home until after the weekend, so I can really knock it on the head.'*

(And as I write out my next cheque to HM Revenue & Customs, I shall try my best not to think of this man in his bed, chasing those elusive last few per cent ...)

It might simply be the case that, despite my tight-fisted refusal to buy organic food, or really to fuss about my children's diet at all – except occasionally to say 'maybe you should eat an apple if there is one, before you finish all those biscuits' – they are (at time of writing) blessed with unusually strong constitutions. Or it might be that, in a household where both earners are self-employed, the suggestion that anyone should stay home in bed is actually laughable – as long as we're functioning at anything above, oh, I don't know (these things are hard to measure), let's say six per cent?

'You *can* stay home,' I say to the children, *slightly impatiently*. 'If you *really* don't feel up to it. It's up to you. *It's your call.* But you'll be very bored and very lonely ... Why don't you sort of *go* to school – and then see how it works out? And if you feel absolutely rotten, then we'll find a way of getting you home again ...'

As a child, I remember being amazed when classmates stayed home simply because they 'weren't feeling very well' or because they 'had a cold'. It seemed incredibly drippy back then. It seems incredibly drippy today. And even harder to comprehend, bearing in mind how many of us now work, and what an impact a child sick at home must have on the mobility and productivity of its working mother.

## Seeing The Doctor

The physical state of any family member needs to be grim indeed if it has driven us to join the snuffling, deadweight inertia of a doctor's surgery.

Christ, they are depressing places. Aren't they though?

First, there's the demoralising period in the reception room, waiting politely to be seen. You never know how long this will last, and yet, inexplicably, it seems rude to ask. Brimming with old, lonely people with no particular place to go, and young, neurotic mothers, hanging around pointlessly for Big Brother to pop their naked babies on weighing scales, it's difficult to remain in the waiting room for long without losing the will to live: thereby rather defeating the purpose of the excursion.

After the Demoralising Period (duration unspecified) there comes the moment – dizzyingly brief – when you and your child are actually allowed in to see the doctor.

*Tappety-tap* at the keyboard, goes the Doc, hardly pausing to look up from his/her computer screen. What-seems-to-be-the-problem? *Tappety-tap* ...

But the sad truth is, when it comes to the usual array of childish (or adult) afflictions, there's rarely much they can do to help. 'If it hasn't cleared up in a few days, then come back,' they say. *Tappety-tap*. And we say, politely gathering our coats, Come on darling! Time to go! Say thank you to the doctor!

And off we waddle home again. Half a morning wasted.

And in a couple of days, lo and behold, the childish affliction clears up.

I tried to beat the system once. Tried to save everyone's time and – in true, guilty-middle-class fashion – to minimise any inconvenience my middle-class family might impose on our sometimes magnificent, sometimes unforgivably complacent NHS, by saving up a handful of minor complaints in the same child before finally carting him to the surgery. We whistled through the first complaint in a matter of seconds. The doctor said the child would grow out of it. As indeed the child did. When I tried to mention the second complaint, the GP held up a hand. It was impossible, he said, for us to continue. Under no circumstances could he deal with two complaints in a single appointment.

'But we've only taken up a minute of your time so far,' I cried.

He shook his head. There were systems. It should have been made clear to us beforehand. If I wanted to discuss a separate complaint, I would have to make a separate appointment.

I didn't bother. I can't even remember now what the complaints were that the doctor was so desperate not to hear about. It was ages ago. Whatever they were, they must have cleared up, as minor afflictions tend to.

GPs, let's face it, are generally (and not necessarily through any fault of their own) very slightly useless. Unless there's something seriously wrong. Or unless you happen to be someone who simply enjoys describing minor health symptoms to health professionals for the hell of it ... And actually, I'm beginning to realise there are plenty of people out there who do – if not describing their own malfunctions, then their children's. In any case, I am not one of them. If an ailment is going to get better anyway, as most do, it's hard to see the point of making a journey to somewhere incredibly depressing to discuss it with someone who almost certainly won't be able to help. Save time – yours, your child's and the doctor's. Take some Calpol/paracetamol – and trot on.

## NHS Helplines

I rang the old helpline once, when the service was still run by nurses and the advice was supposed to be good. It was before we all had the Internet at home. There had been chickenpox at the nursery school. My three-year-old child had a fever and several unpretty blemishes on the skin. I'd not seen chickenpox before and needed the helpline to explain to me what it looked like. So I described the symptoms, blemishes, age of child and explained there had been chickenpox at the nursery school, and so on. After a ten-minute consultation, the woman at the other end (a nurse, I presume) finally delivered her assessment:

'I haven't the foggiest. It might be an STD.'

I took the child to the doctor, who said, 'It's chickenpox. If it hasn't cleared up in a few days, come back.'

*Come on darling!* I said. *Time to go! Say thank you to the doctor!*

And off we waddled home again.

## Other People's Children

Are likely to be fractionally less interesting and more irritating to us than our own, and the younger and more whiny they are, the more adamantly this tends to be the case. Other People's Children do, however, play an important role – no matter what their age – because they often make our own children very happy. Also, from the mistakes they make while visiting our houses, they can throw a useful light on how our own children – so fascinating, fragile and delightful to us – might be slightly annoying when visiting the houses of others.

Other People's Children, I hasten to add (yours, especially) are often genuinely adorable. But they do start from a disadvantage. What we like to call 'confidence' in our own children, can come across in others more like a deluded sense of entitlement.

Children are inclined to be solipsistic at the best of times. They can't help that. Due to being young and inexperienced. But modern parenting, with its 'stop-the-world, our kiddie king is self-expressing' approach, seems, unhelpfully, to encourage their skewed vision rather than attempt to put it right.

Our children have been encouraged to function under the false assumption that every adult in their orbit – with the possible exception of the numerous paedophiles roaming outside every sweetie shop – has their interests, personal comfort and immediate pleasure uppermost in their hearts and minds. Hence the occasional unsolicited bulletins from visiting children, when presented with a plate of food, as to how much they're probably not going to like it.

'I hope s/he likes chicken nuggets,' mothers used to say to me, when they were having one of my children to tea. *'Does s/he like chicken nuggets?* Because if s/he doesn't like chicken nuggets, we can easily bung in a couple of extra sausages. It's no trouble at all! Does s/he like chicken nuggets?'

*'Bloody hell!'* I wanted to cry. *'Does he like Green Eggs and Ham?*

... For heaven's sake, he'll probably like the nuggets. Or maybe he won't – but don't bung in any extra sausages! What do you want to do that for?'

I don't expect much from the children who visit us; they come, they go; they are always welcome. Some are cute – there's an extra-cute one on the landing outside the door as I write this, giggling about stolen biscuits. I'm very fond of some of them, embarrassingly so, my children would probably tell me. In any case, it's a lovely surprise when they grew a little older and engage in conversation. It's a nuisance if, when they're young, they occasionally smash things or finish *all* the biscuits, or stay up half the night, bouncing footballs in the hall. Or making pancakes. Or flooding the bathroom. Or scribbling 'art' on the walls ... Generally, of course, they don't. And if they do, it's not the end of the world. Far from it. It may be a nuisance, but it's also part of the merry chaos of life and – so long as nobody expects anyone to bung in any alternative menus or to do anything for them at all, really, except vacate the telly room and (see 'Sleepovers' on page 162) direct them to the cupboard where we keep the sleeping bags – it's a pleasure to have them round.

However, as they leave the house, trailing empty biscuit tins and pizza boxes behind them, there ought to be some sort of a Green Cross Code for child guests ... Stop. *Look at me.* And say, 'Goodbye and thank you.' It's all I want. In exchange for quite so many biscuits, it seems like a small ask.

## Manners And Charm

Are more or less the same thing and in a civilised world, after an ability to lie (see page 174), are possibly the most vital of all the life skills. As I tell my children. Properly applied, they can ease the path to the moon.

So it's peculiar that it's often the most intensely tended children, with the most perfectionist, most pernickity mothers, who are least aware of this basic but vital truth.

I have lost count of the number of visiting children over the long years, who, when their parents arrive to take them home (see above and indeed below), sweep out of the house without pausing to say thank you. And it *really* pisses me off. Grade 1 in Basic Charm Skills only requires two things: to say please, to say thank you and … okay, three things; to make eye contact, even if it's only for a split second, at the moment of uttering the words.

The child's parent knows to say thank you, and says it on the child's behalf. Sometimes the parent might even make a half-hearted attempt to prompt the child into saying it for themselves: *'Have you got your shoes? Shall we zip up your coat? Did you have a super time? Are you going to say thank you?'* … But when the child inexplicably (because after all, why not?) refuses to oblige, or when they mumble the words in hostile fashion while gazing at the floor, their parents don't pursue it. They roll their eyes. Shrug. Ruffle their horrible little child's hair … *Hey-ho. Kids will be kids!*

And I smile politely, tussling silently with my inner demon, as it urges me to reach for the nearest cricket bat and whack the pair of them over the head.

## Saying 'Playdate'

It's not pretty, is it? We don't say, 'sex date', 'watching-a-movie date' or 'drinking-alcohol date'. In fact, now I think about it, beyond the usual 'Does anyone know the …?' The English don't say 'date' much at all. It's an Americanism: simultaneously formal and coy – on par with 'sleepover'. I am vaguely disappointed with myself for having succumbed to either word. But I have. For the time being. You have to pick your battles.

## Picking Up Children After Playdates

The doorbell rings. You go to answer it and as you do so, you shout up the stairs/along the hallway to the visiting child, 'Darling!' (thereby saving yourself from having to remember which child, exactly, is visiting) 'Your mum is here to fetch you.'

Which bulletin 'Darling', who isn't desperate to leave, either ignores entirely or interprets as an amusing cue to venture deeper, and/or higher into the house, as far as possible from front door and collecting parent. Darling and his/her teatime host (my child) may even (may often) choose to take the hilarious 'I'm-not-going-home' jape further still, and hide in a cupboard, where I think they genuinely believe they will never be found.

So it goes. Children will be children ... And so on.

It wouldn't matter in the least, if only the adults involved could pull together to facilitate a smooth, good-natured and (above all) brisk extraction of child guest, thereby enabling us all to get on with our lives.

But it never happens. Standing in the hallway, we adults are trapped within our mini-tornado of parental niceties – unable to pause the small talk and yell at the children, though we know they will never emerge without our concentrated insistence – for fear of seeming impatient to get away from one another. And so, upstairs, the children giggle and snort and ransack the cupboard: downstairs the minutes tick by with neither party certain how, politely, to draw the situation to its mutually longed-for conclusion.

'Yes, I was pleased they put swimming back to Fridays again ...'

'They seemed to enjoy their visit to the museum, didn't they?'

'I hear poor little Frankie got a bit travel-sick on the coach?'

'He did! But he's fine now. Thank goodness ...'

'*Thank goodness!* That's all right then ...'

'... Are you going away this summer?'

It's an impossible situation for both parties. And though there are always exceptions – the odd, full-throttle Crazy whose solitary mission, it seems, is to set up camp in your hall and to never, ever go away – most parents don't *want* to linger in each other's doorways with no definite end in sight, killing themselves softly with politesse ...

'THIS IS SERIOUS,' as Mr Crow of Pearblossom might

observe. 'This is the sort of thing that somebody will have to do something about.'

And although there's often nothing more pleasant than to spend a few idle moments chewing the cud with a fellow parent, what we need, clearly, are some guidelines. So here goes:

## *Picking Up From Playdates: Code Of Conduct*

1) Chauffeur Parents, arriving to pick up a visiting child, should brief the child in advance of the great event. Preferably in quite a scary way, so that the child definitely absorbs it. A chauffeur Parent might want to say something along the lines of:

> 'If you leave me stranded in that hallway making small talk with [Darling's] parent, while you fart around upstairs hiding in the cupboard, I swear on your father's life that I will never, NEVER come and pick you up from anyone's house, ever again.'

This might work. But it generally doesn't. In which case, further tactics might need to be considered.

2) Chauffeur Parents might consider bringing other children with them to sit in the car, thereby providing a reasonable excuse to chivvy things along in an urgent manner without offending the Host.

3) Chauffeur Parents who bring younger children with them to the door should **hold onto them tightly**, never allowing

them to venture any deeper into the house than where the Host Parent is standing (usually a few feet in front of the door, accidentally on purpose trying to obstruct the route).

4) If the Chauffeur Parent has not been offered a drink within, let's say, the first six and a half minutes ... it's probably an indication that the Host Parent needs to crack on with his or her day. This means that if the Host Parent then offers a drink in the seventh minute, they're doing it on sufferance and out of sheer desperation and **Under No Circumstances** should the Chauffeur Parent accept it. Take the invitation in the spirit in which is was meant, fetch your child and get the hell out of the hallway.

5) Can we all agree that it's okay to yell upstairs at children hiding in cupboards? Host Parents may look embarrassed. They may even look disapproving. But underneath, they'll be celebrating.

6) Chauffeur Parents picking up children in London, or in other places where traffic wardens are known to lurk, can always pretend they have left the car illegally parked. This allows Chauffeur Parents to be very assertive about the extraction, possibly (although this can be awkward) by venturing into the upstairs cupboard to scoop out the wretched child themselves.

7) If visiting child, having finally emerged from the fucking cupboard, announces it now can't find its sports kit/satchel/ sweater ... it is PERFECTLY REASONABLE, not to say ESSENTIAL after a token mini-search for said possessions, for

the Chauffeur Parent to take the child home regardless, with a request that the Host Child bring whatever is missing to school with them the following morning.

8) And that's it. I won't mention the thing about that final moment, when *Chauffeur Parents really ought to ensure that the visiting child looks their host in the eye AND says thank you.* Because I think I've already made the point.

9) But they should.


## *Sleepovers*

Part of family life, and not necessarily the best part. Or, not for adult members. Younger children tend to be too excited ever to go to sleep. Which can be a nuisance. Also they take over the telly room. Also they thud about all night and make the house shake; and make you worry about what you would do if it actually fell down.

Added to which, very occasionally sleepovers just *go wrong*. Children have meltdowns and parents have to be called out to fetch them in the middle of the night. I've once been called out before, which is a bore, and I've once had to make the call, which is worse than a bore: it's really, acutely embarrassing. 'Hello there. Sorry to bother you ... *everything's fine!* It's just that your child is inconsolably miserable in our house, and is begging for you to come and take him home.' So it goes.

On the whole, sleepovers make our children happy. And that

makes us happy. Also, it's lovely to get to know our children's friends. But can I just say ...

Sleepovers do not have to involve freshly laundered duvet covers or bed sheets. Children don't care, *they don't care about those sort of niceties* – so why would we? All they need is a sleeping bag, a mattress if there's one available, or failing that, sofa cushions, or failing that, the carpet. At a stretch, I'm willing to provide junior guests with clean pillow cases. But not if I can get away with it.

It seems to me a perfectly reasonable quid pro quo. When guests have reached an age when they want to behave like stuffy adults – to sit with us over dinner and discuss the Leveson Report (let's say) – then I'll be more than happy to treat them like stuffy adults: mattress, bed, fresh sheets – the works! Until then, they can take over the telly room. They can scatter popcorn and polystyrene balls from their broken beanbags all over the house; they can stay up until 4 a.m., painting their nails and/or playing FIFA 13, and emerge from their rooms at noon in search of breakfast ... All this they can do. So long as it doesn't keep me awake. And so long as the house doesn't actually fall down. And so long as they attempt to clear up at least some of the mess afterwards.

With adult luxuries come adult responsibilities. Or something. Whatever excuse it takes. I'm just saying the children's friends are always welcome. They can stay as often as they like, but I definitely can't be bothered to make them up a bed.

## *Dressing For The Weather*

It's another theme that looms large in the domestic hallways of the northern hemisphere, often played out at tedious length by Chauffeur Parents picking up their children post playdate.

Parents expend vast quantities of energy battling with their children to put on coats they don't want to put on. Or battling with them to do up coats they don't want to do up. Or to pile on hats and scarves and gloves that they don't want piled on. Two things always strike me about this: the saintliness and patience of the parents; and the extreme pointlessness of the exercise.

In any case, as often as not the children are only taking eight short but breezy steps from a hallway to the back of a heated car. It wouldn't matter much, even in a snowstorm, if they made the journey in their underpants. In the olden days, perhaps, before closed-top cars and the invention of penicillin, I can see it made sense to have a more watchful approach to the elements. But these days?

Rather than spending long, dreary moments arguing with children about how hot or cold they might be going to be in the future, it seems more sensible to let them find out for themselves. They have been fitted with their own thermostats, after all.

- If they feel cold, they will almost certainly put on an overcoat!
- And if they feel hot, why, they will probably want to take it off again!

- And if they leave the house without taking a coat, and then find themselves feeling chilly …
  (Drum roll please.)
- *They'll probably choose to take a coat with them next time!*

I dislike telling my children what to do and avoid it wherever possible. It bores me, it irritates them, it forces both parties into antagonistic positions and it forces out of kilter what is meant to be the underlying music of family life – or at any rate for me: namely, pleasure in one another's company.

If a child wants to experiment with T-shirts in January, might as well let them. Chances are, they won't want to experiment for very long.

## Chauffeuring And Public Transport

Children don't get to roam around much any more. They tend to be ferried from temperature-controlled inside space to designated sports field, and back and forth and back again, without being exposed to much of the world in between. And judging by their drab expressions as they gaze out of their mother's automobile windows, it's every bit as boring for them as we might imagine. Presumably it's pretty bloody boring for their mothers, too.

I live in a well-to-do, middle class suburb, full of well-to-do, middle class schools. Come 8.15 a.m. on a weekday morning, the roads around me are chock-a-block with mothers, perched high in juggernaut cars, built to withstand the hazards of the

Alaskan tundra and landmines in Afghanistan, but trundling instead along the dewy London tarmac, from school to rugby pitch, to private tutor to piano lesson ... I stare at the women's faces, flat with ennui, most of them ... And I stare at their children lolling wetly in the back seats, safely strapped in, vacant, silent ...

It seems such a waste of living time! If the mothers told their children to climb out of their air-conditioned safety boxes, and get on the frigging bus – why! – they could spend the traffic jam hours, not strumming the steering wheel to Magicfm, but fine-tuning their Portuguese! Raising money for dolphins! Painting a modern masterpiece!

What's it to me? Nothing at all. It's none of my business. But each morning, as I see them chugging slowly by, I can't help but wonder: *what's the point?*

Nothing, I suppose, could ever be as orderly and secure as a childhood spent strapped into the back seat of an air-conditioned four-wheel-drive. And if her child's safety is a mother's single and solitary goal (though it begs the question: *what's the point of giving a person a life if the person's never allowed to live it?*), then I suppose what better way is there to kill the long hours between breakfast and parentoholic o'clock, than in a nice, slow-moving traffic jam?

## *Kiddie Safety Kit*

Don't like writing this. Feels like I'm tempting fate.

Terrible things happen. Children get kidnapped, and run

over, and murdered, and crushed, and stolen, and mugged, and stabbed, and …

*Holy fuck, STOP!*

Nevertheless …

Of course it depends, once again, whether we believe that safety is the be-all and end-all of existence. And for some people I'm guessing it really must be. But I think they're wrong.

As a child, growing up in the country, my cousin and I used to ride a lot together. My mother and aunt, who lived next door to each other, insisted we wore hard hats; and I think at some point during my youth the wearing of riding hats might even have become required by law. Or maybe our mothers only told us that, because they thought it might encourage us to keep the wretched things on.

But the trouble with hard hats – they make your head itch. So we would put the hats on as we rode past the house, just in case either mother was looking out, and then, as soon as we were out of sight, take them off and hide them under a tree.

Because it's hard to beat the feeling of total elation – that wild sense of being alive – of travelling at full pelt, slightly out of control and slightly frightened, with the wind blowing in your hair. And to this day, those childhood rides over the hills remain among my happiest, most exhilarating memories.

There's a private nursery school close to where I live today. Its pupils often travel from their mothers' juggernauts, up the longish garden path to the nursery school door via miniature scooters, which have been handed to them by their solicitous mothers from the boots of their mega-cars. And I notice – more and more – that the majority of the children are only allowed to scoot that safe little journey after their mothers have jammed a sodding great helmet onto their heads, and buckled a chin protector tight around their necks.

Mothers fear for their children. We always have and always will – but our natural aversion to risk, fed as it is by the manufacturers of increasingly preposterous 'safety products', fed too by the fearmongering in newspapers and on television, and fed by ourselves and by each other, seems to me to be teetering on madness. We can never render our children's world one hundred per cent safe and secure, not without sucking out every ounce of mystery and magic. Protecting our children to the nth degree isn't good parenting. Not really. I don't think so. I think it's selfish parenting.

How and when do we let go? Hell, I don't know! Each to our own. Only it seems sometimes, in our increasingly neurotic need to make everything orderly and perfect for our children, to make no mistakes, to put not a foot wrong and to keep all and any risk at bay, that we forget to introduce them (and ourselves) to the pleasures of simply *living* – not even dangerously: but just living at all.

## Godparents

I think I've fallen out with one of my oldest friends. His son is my godson, and I forgot his birthday; which misdemeanor, by the way, I do not count as serious. If it counts as a misdemeanor at all. In any case, I was abroad at the time of the offence. His father and I hadn't been in touch for many months, and the date, never that deeply imprinted, had slipped my mind completely. I received a text from the child's father at about teatime – no words, no message, just a photograph of the hapless godson holding a birthday balloon. Quite funny? Oh maybe it is. But at the time, I was furious.

It's an honour to be asked to be a godparent. Of course. It's wonderful to think that, in years to come, I might be able to help out said friend's child in some way that the parents perhaps cannot. And so on. But I think I made a mistake in the early days, when I accepted the role. I should have made it clear: godparenting means different things to different people.

To me, it means:

I'll give him money when I see him. I may even leave him some cash in my will (unlikely, unless I make a fortune, I have children of my own). I might send him a present every now and then. If he ever needs a place to kip, a friendly ear, some introductions in the world of publishing. Yup – I'm here to serve. And, may I add, with pleasure. I look forward to knowing the child better in the years to come.

But when a relationship becomes nothing more than an inflexible checklist of chores, formalities and to-dos:

I send a present on this day.

You send a thank you letter on that ...

... it's not a relationship, it's a pointless, joyless, grinding bore.

## *Thank You Letters*

I wrote a newspaper article a while back, in which I suggested that children should no longer be made to write thank you letters. Remembering how much I had hated writing the bloody things myself and what a doubly bitter blow it had been to receive a duff present, knowing I would later be required to drum up pen, paper and gushing enthusiasm, no matter what, I observed that thank you letters from children had always struck me, less as a mark of youthful good manners and more as an adult exercise in a) competitive mothering (see how quickly my well-trained child writes to you) and b) revenge:

*I have inconvenienced myself by buying and wrapping this present for you. In return, no matter how little you like the present, and, in fact, how little time I spent choosing it for you, you must inconvenience yourself (to the power of a thousand) by writing to tell me how much you adore it.*

The process runs counter to the true spirit of giving. Doesn't it? Of course it does!

Added to which, knowing (as we all must) what agonies a child is likely to have suffered in the writing of the wretched thing, it's hard not to read them without a lingering sense of shame.

Thank you letters are hell to write, often very dull to read, and above all, a nightmare to bully your children into writing.

In any case, the article provoked an extraordinarily angry response. You might have imagined I had written, denying the Holocaust. In fact, I received so many outraged emails that after a few days any correspondence with subject headline words including, 'thank you', 'letter', 'angry and disappointed' or 'people like you don't deserve to have children' were magically filtered directly into junk.

Of course, people who go to the effort of writing very angry letters to newspapers are already a self-defining group; in a carefree moment we might refer to them as 'lunatics'. Loonies they might be, nevertheless it takes specific hot topics to bring them out of the woodwork, and 'children's thank you letters', it transpires, pushes all the buttons. Any political party wanting to get elected might bear it in mind. Forget about the biscuits. They really only need to make two promises:

1) Not to move the clocks forward in winter.

2) To make Thank You Letter Writing Skills a compulsory element on a new National Curriculum.

## Swearing

I was walking along the street with my two-and-a-half-year-old son, many moons ago, when we bumped into a neighbour. The neighbour and I stopped to chat, which, as any child would tell you, was annoying of us. My son tugged on my arm and waited impatiently for the conversation to finish. Finally, the neighbour bent down to address him.

'HELLO THERE LITTLE FELLOW!' he said, in conventional child-friendly tones. 'HOW ARE WE TODAY? ARE WE OFF TO THE SHOP WITH MUMMY THEN?'

And why, indeed, so we were!

It wasn't a difficult question. I had every confidence my son could deal with it himself, so I said nothing, and only prepared to wallow and bask in the inevitable cuteness of his reply c But it didn't come. To my dismay, he said nothing at all. Instead, he gave a small, fey whimper and hid behind my leg.

'IS MUMMY GOING TO BUY YOU SOME SWEETIES?' the neighbour persevered. 'I EXPECT YOU'D LIKE THAT! WOULDN'T THAT BE SUPER?'

And indeed, yes, it would have been super! But he uttered nothing – not a word. Just gave another sad, bored whimper, teetering on a fully fledged blub.

The neighbour soon lost interest. I apologised for my goofy little son, and the lad and I continued on our journey.

'What happened there?' I asked him, when we were out of earshot. 'Why didn't you answer the neighbour?'

He shrugged.

'Have you forgotten what you're meant to say to grown-ups when they say hello to you? What are you supposed to say?'

He replied, 'I'm supposed to say "Hello".'

'Exactly!' I cried triumphantly. 'That's exactly right! And what *aren't* you supposed to do when a grown-up tries to make conversation with you?' (The correct answer to which, clearly was, 'Cling onto my mother's leg and whimper.')

He thought about it.

'I'm pretty sure you know the answer,' I persevered. 'What *don't* you do when a grown-up tries to make conversation with you?'

'I think,' he said finally, 'I don't say "Fuck".'

It was a golden moment for me; a moment of intense maternal pride.

Close students of this very important text may already have noticed that its author swears quite a lot. There are times, I find, when only a swear word will satisfy. Besides, I read somewhere (recentstudieshaveshown) that the act of swearing releases chemicals into the blood (or possibly the brain?) that have a soothing effect on the body, similar to painkillers ... or was it tranquillisers ... or maybe it was laughing gas? In any case, I swear because it pleases me, because I know it teases, and because, when deployed with sufficient chutzpah, some of the best curse words have a magnificently punchy ring to them. And it does the heart good, from time to time, to get one's lips (and keyboard) around them. I swear in front of the children, always have and always will. Partly, as an – admittedly infantile – but strangely satisfying rebellion against the oppressive Gods of Propriety and Tastefulness who rule the world of nicely-nicely parenting ... I say *partly* because now that I think about it, it may be the only reason. Or the main reason.

Give me moment.

All right. Well in fact, that aside ...

Some attitudes, I suppose we inherit.

I never did much alter my vocabulary for the children, nor any other aspect of the way I communicate. I'm not sure that it ever even occurred to me. My parents didn't do it for my siblings and me. They never patronised us. Never used special, kiddie-friendly words or voices. Always talked, often swore, and assumed that at some point, if we were sufficiently interested, we would catch on. And it was good. Excellent, even. It kept us on our toes. In this it has always felt natural to do the same. Long words, complicated ideas and uncomfortable subject matter – peppered with curse words where necessary – have generally been the order of every day.

Because things are *there* to be learned, are they not? *Everything* is there to be learned, and once learned, to be exploited intelligently.

My two-and-a-half-year-old son understood the rules of engagement. Bless his goofy socks. Knowing stuff is good; knowing when and where (not) to apply the knowledge is even better. Don't say 'fuck' to people who will find it shocking. But own that word, and understand – if you find yourself short of laughing gas – that it's sometimes a useful one to call upon.

## *Lying*

How lovely to see you!
I love my job.
I love your mother.
I love you.
That was delicious.

I voted Green.
I called but I think your mobile must have been off.

I can't afford it.
I can afford it.
I remember it well.
It was in the sale.
I haven't got any change.

Sorry, I'm busy that night.
Luckily, I'm not busy that night.
I don't really smoke.
I wish I could but I can't.
You look lovely.
Your children are adorable.
We'd love to come.
What a beautiful service!
Honestly, I really don't mind.

Horrible traffic.
I assumed you knew.
The email must have gone astray.
There wasn't any reception.
We're putting everything we have behind it.
I'm in a meeting.
That took me *hours*.

He's in a meeting.
I'm sick in bed.
I cooked it myself.
Your call is important to us.
I can't hear you – you're breaking up.

There's someone at the door.
My alarm didn't go off.
Of course I was in.
I'm on my way.
I left half an hour ago.
Only two glasses, Officer.
I completely forgot!
It came out of the blue.
I did not inhale.

It's going really well.
Nothing is the matter.
No.
Yes.
We've almost completely sold out.
It wasn't my fault.
I wish I could help you.
It's not company policy.
I'm so excited.
It's just not possible.
That's my highest offer.
He started it.

No, I don't think you're stupid.
I've already checked.
Yes, I am certain.
I had no idea.
That's a lie!
I have to rush.

We'll be sad to lose you.
I haven't breathed a word.
There's nothing more I can do.

I've never had Botox.
I don't believe in diets.
I loved that book.
I definitely locked the door.
I do understand.
You had it last.
You're not fat.
I am listening.

You were brilliant.
I was offended.
I wasn't offended
That's not funny.
That is funny.
I'm definitely not giving up trying.
How interesting.

We never have sex any more.
We have sex the whole time.
That was fantastic.
I did not have sexual relations with that woman.

It's peculiar, isn't it, how adults take such a ferociously dim view of their children lying, when we spend so much time lying ourselves? We lie – and are lied to – so much, we hardly bother to notice it. In fact, lying is the cement that holds our ludicrous adult world together. And I don't mean what, in our mealy-mouthed way, we call 'white' lies. I mean lies of every hue and every colour. We would be lost without them.

So it seems to me that the sooner children learn how to lie efficiently, the better their chances of survival in this dishonest world.

I wonder if parents hate to be lied to, not because lying is wrong (we're on a weak wicket there), but because the moment a child lies, s/he reclaims a little of their birthright, their power as a separate individual. A lying child crosses what was always an unsustainable 'boundary' and steps into a lawless world of their own creation, of which the child is master, and over which a parent can have no control.

I don't like it when my children lie to me – obviously. It makes me feel ostracised. And it makes me worry about what they may be trying to hide. On the other hand, I have to acknowledge that it takes a certain gumption to do it, a refusal to kowtow to my authority. It demonstrates a drive towards self-ownership, independence and personal survival, which, whether we like it or not, are all vital ingredients for a successful adulthood. And even if lying ought not be a skill to be overtly applauded (because in a perfect world we would all tell each other how fat we looked in those trousers, how disgusting our cooking is, and exactly whom we screwed, how, where and when), the act of lying – as distinct from whatever is being lied about – isn't something to be entirely discouraged.

## To Lie Or Not To Lie?

Whereas I expect to lie to other adults almost as a matter of course; and whereas I expect other adults to lie to me, also as a matter of course; and whereas I also expect to be lied to by my children, I try *on the whole* to avoid lying to them. Partly because – obviously – if they can't trust their mother not to feed them bullshit, who the hell can they trust in this bullshit-sodden world? Partly because it seems to be counter-productive. I want my children to be the wisest they can be.

Why then, except in specific and exceptional circumstances (we all need some privacy), would I want to fool them with information I know to be false?

## Father Christmas

Consistency – like honesty – can be overrated. Some things are worth lying about.

He's more often referred to as Santa on the telly. To me, the name 'Santa' conjures everything that is most disheartening about the Christmas season: fat, smirking paedos wearing blusher. And all that. Coca-Cola ads. Mums going to Iceland ...

Father Christmas, on the other hand, seems like a good sort.

However, there is *only one* Father Christmas. He or she tips up just once a year, sometime after midnight, pissed and bumping into things. All the others, especially those that require parents to stand in line in shopping centres where there is no natural light source, are slightly creepy, intensely depressing and should climb back into their sleighs and Jingle Bell (Batman smells) jingle back to hell.

## Children's Presents And The Annual Scrum

In the run-up to Christmas, the newspapers are filled with stories about parents searching slavishly through crowded shops in pursuit of that last available hot toy of the season. This year, I note, it being Christmas time, the toy we were being told every child will have a nervous breakdown without, is an interactive Furby: a robotic, furry creature that communicates – not just with our children, but with others of its kind, and possibly (could it get any better?) with an iPad. The Furby, which comes in a range of colours, costs £59.99 at Argos.

Hey ho. I can imagine it might be the source of some small amusement for an hour or two before the batteries run out. But I'm pretty sure my children will continue to thrive without it. If I happen to see one, I shall act distracted and quickly look the other way.

## Squabbling Children

A friend of mine spent a long winter weekend alone with her two sons a few years ago. The little boys squabbled incessantly. And it's funny, isn't it. Sometimes, for hours at a time, you can simply tune out and leave them to it. 'Get off – You didn't – I did – Ow! – Give me that – Fuck off.'

(Don't swear.)

'He started it – I started – You started – That's a lie – I thought of it – Give me that – Fuck off.'

(Don't swear.)

'Ow!'

… We can tune out to the point where we barely register it at all: a background hum on a par with the kettle. And then, quite suddenly, it becomes intolerable: the lack of creativity in their dialogue, the lack of generosity, the sheer boredom that emanates from their voices … And we snap.

So my friend snapped. On a cold, dark February evening. They were in the kitchen, which opened out, via a large glass door, onto a high-walled, rain-soaked London garden. She shoved them out there, in the pissing rain, 'Go out there and fight!' she said. 'Go on! Get fighting! You can come in when you've fought each other so hard you just can't fight any more. GO ON! FIGHT! FIGHT!' She locked the glass door, and the two boys – astonished by this turn of events – immediately forgot their beef with one another. They pressed their noses against the glass sliding doors and begged to be let back in.

She ignored them. Returned to her work. Every now and then, she would look up from her computer, notice them knocking pathetically on the glass, and order them to start fighting again.

'You're not fighting enough. Do some fighting – FIGHT each other – Why aren't you fighting? GET ON WITH IT! FIGHT.'

But the boys didn't want to fight any more. After a while, quite a while, I may add (she had a lot of work to catch up on), she unlocked the door and let them come back in again. And they didn't exchange a cross word with each other for a week.

## Children Unattended

Lots of bossy laws about this. Not sure what they are, and don't intend to find out. Better off not knowing. (A bit like not owning a thermometer, actual numbers only tend to create panic.) Much better to trust instinct. As it is, we all have a pretty good idea under what circumstances it feels safe to leave our children unattended: at what age, where, and for how long. Only watch out who you tell. There are some heavyweight busybodies out there, often in places you least suspect, and they are only waiting to get people like – well, me – into trouble.

It's a wonderful thing when you first realise you can start to leave your children on their own, even if it's only to go to the shop to stock up on milk. It's like a second adolescence – footloose for all of a hundred yards, though no, never quite fancy-free. But even so. It's hard to beat.

Leave the telly on – and the chances are the children won't even notice you're gone.

## Police

They come to talk to our children at school, of course. Along with the nice people from ChildLine, and the fire brigade, too:

who send children home with a fire safety checklist for their parents. My youngest daughter came home with one last week. Full of fear and enthusiasm.

Good for them. I suppose. Or something. There's a house fire and a family burned alive about once a week in the news, isn't there? Although more often than not, it's a stepfather-plus-arson affair. Never mind. The girl's nervous. She wants to know why we've disabled the fire alarm. Someone, somewhere, had better track down some batteries.

It's the police who have the uphill battle when it comes to winning over our children's hearts and minds. Not just in the badlands, but here and there, and in the most middling of middle-class suburbs, too.

There's a law (for example) which limits the number of passengers allowed to travel in one car. It's a law which is stuck to religiously by some, and broken on a regular basis by everyone else, because there are times – quite a lot of them – when the law is inconvenient. (A nursery school teacher in South Africa took it a little far recently, when she was pulled over for squeezing nineteen pre-schoolers into the back of her little hatchback, on an outing to a nearby playground. Bless her.)

There's another law which requires children under 12 or smaller than 135cm (excluding their shoes) to sit on 'booster' seats; and another about child restraints, front seats and airbags; and almost certainly another that forbids them from travelling in the one place, mysteriously, that they most long to travel, namely in the boot. As a result of this plethora of minor regulations, I think many of us, when ferrying children hither and thither, do so with a vague assumption that one law or another is almost certainly being broken.

And though I don't know of a single parent (except one on Twitter) who went to the trouble of buying the booster seats for 12-year-olds when that law was introduced, nor – to be fair to the polce – of any parent to have been prosecuted or even pulled over for failing to use one, children remain only too aware that their presence in cars is subject to a mass of regulation. And even if their own parents are law-abiding, Dettox-brandishing, Thudguard-dependent neurotics, at some time or other they will have found themselves in a car with other parents who aren't. They will have been driven in an overstuffed, under-boosted car, to a party somewhere, sometime. And they will be familiar with the driver's frantic cry:

'AAAARRRGHH! POLICE! QUICK! EVERYONE – FOR CHRIST'S SAKE, DUCK!'

And they tend to know the drill.

I think it's wonderful. I think it's a great leap forward for civilisation that our claustrophobic, safety-obsessed, impossibly risk-averse culture has inadvertently bred a generation of children who feel comfortable waving aside the sillier, fussier points of personal safety law. You may not agree with me. It doesn't really matter. Either way, we are where we are. Our children understand that sometimes the law is an ass. And that some laws are made to be broken.

## Punishment

Is for institutions. In family life, it seems perverse. Life is difficult enough. The idea of devising extra ways to make it even more difficult, and for the people we love most in the world, goes against common sense, against loving instinct, against human nature itself! Or certainly, against mine.

In a court of law there's no love lost between the punisher and punished, and no suggestion, nor even the slightest hope, that the two parties have a shared goal, let alone that they might in some way (to coin that unfashionable phrase), be all in it together. It's different for families.

Charm, luck, imagination, negotiation, good manners and, yes, the height and colour of the sky, determine how we respond to one another's actions. In private family life there's something chilling about punishment delivered cold.

## Drugs

Have I ever taken any, the children asked recently, before they realised how interminable and earnest my answer would be. They haven't asked again since.

What are we supposed to say? I hadn't really thought it through until the question sat there between us. Somehow, out of the mix of concern, hatred of the usual, useless humbug, and perhaps even, *ahem*, enjoyment of the sound of my own voice, I came up with the following response.

185

Have I taken drugs? Of course I have. Did I enjoy them? Well of course I did … if drug-taking wasn't enjoyable, then why would so many people go to the trouble and risk of doing it in the first place?

When they asked me which drugs, when and why, I swear I numbed them with my windbag honesty. The highs and lows, the pros and cons of my own limited experience. And topped and tailed it all with the story of my brilliant, joyful friend, with whom I picked blackberries as a child, and built bonfires in the woods … who died of a heroin overdose, all alone, choking on her own vomit. *Every mummy should have such a friend!* I am grateful to her.

Who knows if children can ever really absorb the horror of it? Who knows if sharing the story with them will do any good at all? I don't suppose anything I have to say will make the slightest difference when the moment comes. They will be with friends, and I, and my long-dead friend, will be far from their minds … but the knowledge just might – perhaps – leave behind a small residue of caution … and as they say at Tesco, every little helps.

Or maybe it doesn't help. Fuck. I don't know. Only I know I don't want to insult their curiosity by fobbing them off with po-faced non-answers.

Also, by the way, I don't see how *any* parent can take a thunderer's stance on this particular matter. If they've never tried drugs, then clearly they don't know what they're talking about and their opinions on the matter are valueless. And if they have tried them – no matter how little or how much –

then they will at least understand something of the attraction. And until a parent can acknowledge that, then the posture, as we say in yoga (Approach Drugs with Great Care), hasn't even begun.

# Schooldays

## *Nursery School*

Funny how important it seemed to be to get the children into the best one, or rather, the one everyone else, somewhat randomly (it always struck me), agreed was 'the best'. Because looking back at them all now, years later, the ones I looked round and didn't apply for, and the ones I fought and grovelled to get my children into ... I can hardly tell them apart. Lots of little tables and scruffy boxes of well-used toys; a handful of kindly teachers (except for you, Miss B); a classroom filled with small children to entertain and befriend one another ... and a bonus point for a pet rabbit.

A nursery school, above all, is somewhere to dump the toddler for a couple of hours each morning, so that the child's mother can begin to remember what it was like to be human again. The sort of human who, for example, is free to amble to the lavatory, without a ten-minute hazard analysis of leaving a toddler alone in a sitting room unattended.

Some nursery schools may have shinier toys, of course. Some may teach your child to write their name earlier than others. (But what's the rush?) Some may advertise their smartness with twee-looking gingham overall uniforms. But when you get down to it, they're all *pretty much* the same. The only thing that really matters is that it's nearby. As near as possible. Those precious three hours spin past, faster than time ever has or ever will again. Spend it travelling backwards and forwards to the 'best' nursery school, and you may yet run out of time for that longed-for impulse trip to the lavatory. You certainly won't have time to let the milkman in.

## Having A Little Cry

I have forgotten when Mummy is officially expected to do this … when a child starts at nursery, or when a child leaves it to go to school? Personally, I don't remember 'having a little cry' at either end of this incredibly minor chapter in a child's life. Except perhaps a brief smarting of relief, when I realised I would never again have to be polite to the dreaded sourpuss, Miss B.

However, on the first and last days of nursery school, I do remember there being a lot of talk of mummies and their tears.

*'I had a little cry.'*

It's what we said to each other, while pulling mysteriously soppy faces. I'm still not sure what we were supposed to be crying about.

I wonder if anyone did?

Yes. And while I'm on the subject of things that were meant to be enjoyable, carefree mini-rites of passage …

## Children's Birthday Parties

They've become laughably competitive. In my rich, middle class corner of the world, the extent to which neurotic parents will go to outshine one another is beyond parody. I know of children whose parents have flown half a class of children to Euro Disney for the weekend; I know of one ten-year-old whose parents rented a suite at the Savoy for all the girls in the class, and booked a couple of professional make-up artists as entertainment for a 'make-over-'n'-sleep-over party'. I know of children whose parents have rented out entire cinemas, so that the children can watch a special early screening of a film that's yet to be released. All of which, I realise, is extreme – a symptom of the peculiar wealth still sloshing around in London private schools. Bring on the revolution.

Nevertheless, the drive to make children's birthday parties more special, more memorable, more extravagant than anyone else's, is not only a frailty of the extortionately rich. And I promised myself when I set out to write this book, that I would never use the words 'in my day' (it was tougher) 'and we were perfectly all right'.

However.

In my day, we had a few people round, some jelly and Hula Hoops, a pass the parcel (with A SINGLE present in the centre, not one at every layer), a game of pin the tail on the donkey, some musical statues and birthday cake. *Thank you for having me*. Time to go home (maybe with a balloon). And that was it. And it was better than perfectly all right. It was bloody wonderful. Especially the jelly.

It takes nerves of steel to pull off anything so simple today. Even basic birthday parties at home (as opposed to the ones in cripplingly expensive theme parks, paintball arenas, etc.) seem to involve kiddie-friendly party wranglers in embarrassing kiddie-friendly clown clothes @ £100-200 a pop ... And what with the themed party bags, matching, themed party stationery, themed bloody birthday cake – the cost of these little get-togethers can skyrocket.

It's madness, I tell you!

Why do we do it? God only knows.

How do we stop? Well now.

We just *stop*.

I gave a fourth birthday party for one of my children, several years ago. I had 'organised' the party myself – *sans* the £200 entertainer – and I'll be honest, it was chaos. Anarchy. I was desperate. Nobody wanted to play the party games. Or sit down to tea, or to do whatever else it was they were meant to be doing. A girlfriend of mine, there for moral support – who didn't have children at the time – said, 'Oh just put some music on and tell them to dance.' So I did. And the children danced ... and danced ... and danced. And then they had some birthday cake. And then they went home and lived happily ever after.

Small children couldn't care less what's laid on, so long as something is, and they're at the centre of it. So long as there's jelly. And a couple of prizes. And everyone sings 'Happy Birthday' and makes them feel special. Older children may not want musical bumps and jelly, but whatever they do want, if it's expensive, it can be done with a single friend, not in a bloody great group. Apart from the fact that such lavish parties are unnecessary and unaffordable, I think they're gross. Because spoilt children are gross. And so are their stupid parents.

And so, by the way, is this: though for different reasons.

A friend of mine has just forwarded me a party invitation addressed to her six-year-old son. Party guests are advised to bring 'strong shoes or wellies' as they will be walking 'approximately 150 metres' between feasting table and small park, for the party games.

*'We will be enough adults,'* the birthday boy's mother adds at the bottom of the invitation, *'to satisfy OFSTED requirements for adult to child ratio for the walk down ☺.'*

Oh! It's all so joyless! It's so cautious! It's so inelegant! It's so unutterably *pathetic*. What has become of us all? Who gives a flying fuck what satisfies OFSTED? It's a private party! And it makes me want to emigrate.

## Going Private

It's an unfair system. We all know it's unfair. And inevitably it brings out the humbug in us because where there is a clash of interests between, let's say, a better, fairer, more decent world, and the welfare of our own children ... The contest is over before it's even started. Our crazy education system makes almost anyone interested or involved in it feel angry, neurotic, guilty ... and a bit bitter. The difference between the private and state sectors seems, in general, from my uncomfortable and precarious position up here in the ivory tower, to be wide.

Maybe the free schools will help to bring about change. Who knows? Judging by the 2,000-strong queue that circled the block when I attended the open day for our local free school (not local enough, unfortunately), it's what a lot of parents are pinning their hopes on, from both sides of this fractious divide.

I have nothing much to add to this non-debate, this unhappy state of affairs. But in the meantime, can I just very quickly point out, that nobody *enjoys* paying bloody school fees. A lot of people who educate their children privately do it because they can just about afford it, and therefore feel duty-bound to try.

Meeting such astronomical bills each year, term after term, shapes working lives and sleepless nights. The suggestion that parents go to such lengths out of social snobbery (in a country so riddled with class hatred), strikes me as a bit silly. Ditto, the suggestion that middle-class parents who *don't* choose to send their children to independent schools are in some way morally superior. Ditto, that those fortunate enough to have been educated in what is, lest we forget, an independent sector, internationally envied, aped and respected, are in some way less valid people as a result of that.

Only in this guilt-ridden, humbug-riddled country would the fact of a man having been educated at what is considered to be one of best schools in the world, be a serious reason not to elect him as its leader.

## School Snobbery

I should add, however, that I met an idiotic woman recently, who was so desperate to get her child into a fashionable nursery school, she had her husband call the school's admissions office from her maternity hospital bed.

## Conversations About Schools

Remember how boring everyone used to be about property prices? It seems a lifetime ago now. People barely mention them any more. It's one of the great blessings – possibly the only blessing – of the world economic meltdown: a fantastic opportunity to find something more interesting to talk about.

If only.

There's a wonderful scene in Luc Besson's 1985 movie *Subway*, in which Isabelle Adjani, having sat sullenly through the first half of a bourgeois dinner party, can suddenly not endure her neighbour's complacent conversation for a moment longer. *'Stop!'* [she interrupts her] *'Racontez tout ça à votre voisin, parce que moi je n'en ai rien à branler de vos conneries.'*

(Loosely: Tell that to someone else because I don't give a fuck for your bullshit.)

I think longingly of that line every time local parents get together, and, like clockwork, our conversation turns, so earnest and so respectable – as if our lives depended on it – to the subject of Which School? Specifically, the pros and cons of different (private) schools in our area. All of which are excellent. Lucky us. None of which, finally, will be the deciding factor in how our children's lives and personalities pan out. 'This one offers Mandarin!' … 'I wasn't terribly impressed by the ICT department in that one.' … 'The other one has superb sporting facilities!'

Jolly good show. Smug bores.

So what shall we talk about now?

## Faith School Hoop-Jumping

'If you set up a school,' as John Prescott, former deputy prime minister, once famously said, 'and it becomes a good school, the great danger is that everyone wants to go there.' Bless him. Indeed they do. People sneer at 'pushy middle-class parents', who pretend to be religious to get their children into faith schools. But I don't see why. (I tried, by the way. Years ago. I may yet try again.) Faith schools tend to be good schools. Most of us will do and say whatever we can if we feel it will help our children. Pull a holy face and take communion? Suck up to the local priest? Good God. Why ever not?

And if, in the early years, your Catholic-educated child happens to ask, for example, if you *really and truly* believe in transubstantiation? Well now, it depends how strongly you feel about these matters ... Perhaps divert her attention with a nice little story about Father Christmas.

## *Children's Homework*

The point of it, I thought, was for children to practise what they had been taught at school and to learn to work on their own. I don't mind being called over to help if a child gets stuck (although Google is often a safer bet), but beyond the age of seven, let's say, I am bewildered by the suggestion – not, I hasten to add, that my children would ever be flopsy enough to make it – that I might be expected to sit down at the kitchen table with them, night after night, and nurse them through each task and question.

Children are often asked to design posters for their homework. Which is fun. One morning several years ago, I was accompanying my child – then about nine years old and clutching homework poster – to the classroom. She had been quite proud of it when she finished it the previous evening, and I, too, had thought it was a masterpiece. But as we drew closer to her form room, several of her classmates sauntered by, many of them with beautiful, symmetrical, info-packed, plastic-laminated artwork tucked neatly under their little arms.

I said to my child, 'Oh my God – have you seen? Your poster is crap!'

It was, too. In comparison. There was no denying it. And yet I knew she had tried reasonably hard. I had spotted her out of the corner of my eye, printing and cutting and folding and sticking in the far corner of the kitchen, while I was tapping away. Until then I had always assumed she was a smart girl ... But her poster was useless! Was she a dunce then, after all? Was it possible? The evidence was certainly pointing that way. We were both extremely sad.

So sad (in my case), I was later moved to ask the teacher.

'Is my girl a duffer?' I asked. 'Is she as dozy as her poster seems to imply?'

The teacher said the girl was doing just fine.

And advised me to advise my child not to be disheartened. Half of the posters, he said, will have been done by the mothers. 'It's always very obvious when the mothers are doing it for them. And obviously that gets reflected in the final mark.'

My child was not a sandwich short of a picnic after all! It was just that she did her own homework!

So.

One less thing to worry about.

Which isn't to say (I should add, with a small but noticeable clearing of throat) that homework efforts don't need to be policed ... and I can see that when it comes to academic work, some children might benefit from a slightly less libertarian approach ... Nevertheless, there is a difference between checking a child's homework when it's finished and kicking up a stink if it's useless (boring, but possibly essential), and actually sitting down and doing the homework for and with them. (Boring, time-consuming, feeble and, I suspect, counter-productive.)

After all, you can't take your Mummy into the exam room, can you? You cannot. And thank goodness for that.

## *Tutors*

People lie about their personal tutor habit almost as much as they lie about their sex lives. Like nannies, and other domestic helpers, tutors are a sort of dirty secret of the middle class, whose existence is often blatantly denied by the parents who employ them. Don't know why. Unless of course one of the parents is a politician, or one of the thousands who claim to take a moral stand against the iniquities of private education.

The other thing worth remembering about tutors, by the way, is that some are more cynical than others and that, @ £50/hour (approx), their livelihood depends on parents feeling insecure and worried about their children's education. If, as has happened to me, a particular tutor makes a habit of whipping you up into a frenzy of concern, just breathe deeply (I forgot to do this), and remember: things may not be half as bad as they say.

Far from it, in fact. Children develop at different rates. And that's okay. Isn't it? I think so.

It's a grubby business, earning a living. And tutors have mortgages too.

## *Sports Kit (Lost And Found)*

*SOME* sports teachers seem to think parents have a bottomless pit of cash; that we trudge from our breakfast tables to our desks each morning specifically and exclusively so we can earn the money to spend on differently emblemed, subtly different football sweaters, rugby shirts and hockey fleeces. It's infuriating, and since *SOME* sports teachers seem to love nothing more than handing out punishments to students who turn up without the correct emblem on the *correct sock*, there's not much to be done about it, except to cough up and buy the wretched stuff. Work a bit harder. Eat a little less. Sell the car. Switch off the central heating. Sell a kidney ... I've made the point.

At the start of each year ... all right, maybe at the start of every other year ... *certainly* at the start of a new school, I make every effort to kit out the children with (almost) everything on the equipment list. And if, by some fluke, they've managed to hold onto a particular item long enough to grow out of it (ha bloody ha), then it seems unreasonable not to buy them a replacement – at some point.

Beyond that, they're pretty much on their own.

Children can't help losing kit. Like teenagers lose cigarette lighters. Remember? Lighters came and lighters went. They did the rounds, disappeared into a friend's pocket, and then into another friend's pocket, only to reappear in your own pocket – as if by magic – a month or so later. The system worked so long as everybody contributed a lighter to the cycle every now and then.

Sensible children (and more pragmatic parents) have long since worked out a similar system with sports kit.

Of course, there will always be other parents, who want to fuss, who are determined to keep track of their poor children's incomplete equipment no matter what. So they whip themselves up into a froth and spin, and turn themselves into a laughing stock, sending out frantic round robins to classmate parents asking us to check kit bags for their children's missing kit.

It's certainly one way of approaching the problem.

The other is to remain aloof. Where there is a school full of children, there will always be plenty of lost kit floating around. And so long as we (parents) have, at some point, contributed equivalent kit to the Lost Property Mountain, it seems perfectly reasonable for our offspring to borrow from that mountain as the need arises. It's an elegant system – one of communism and recycling – which I think many parents support, if only tacitly. Everyone saves money, thanks to the array of clothes sizes always available in said mountain. It means children don't have to have nervous breakdowns each time they lose an item of clothing ... sports teachers never need to find out, and, just for once ... parents don't need to get their wallets out.

Is my daughter wearing somebody else's netball sweatshirt? Almost certainly. Is somebody else using her hockey stick? Without a doubt. The good news is, it doesn't matter. Nobody has to yell at anybody else and nobody has to get yelled at.

## Nits

Hedrin. It doesn't stink, and it actually works. But it costs a fortune. With all the money I've spent over the years on bottles of Hedrin, I could probably buy – well now, definitely a holiday somewhere. Possibly a house in the south of France. In fact, a few years ago, so desperate was I for a lice-and-nit-free household, I forwent the bloody Hedrin and attended *en famille* a special nit-terminating 'salon', where an army of nit-killers dressed, oddly, like astronauts, put specially adapted Hoovers to our heads. Sitting with her children at the Hoover beside mine, by the way, was Thandie Newton, Famously Beautiful Movie Star ... that's correct ... because it turns out even Famously Beautiful Movie Stars get nits off their children! Which, if you ask me, already destigmatises them a bit. Doesn't it?

Anyway the point is, no matter what you do, no matter how much money and effort and astronauts and bloodlust you throw into the eradication project, someone in a classroom somewhere ALWAYS has nits. And one way or another, lice, like the Terminator, will Be Back. It's an unwinnable war. And there comes a moment when you have to ask yourself: is it worth the fight?

The first time I encountered lice was before I had children of my own. A young niece or nephew had left a few drowned bodies in the bottom of their grandparents' bathtub one day. I kicked up an almighty fuss. Those little drowned insects – synonymous to me, back then, with dirt and rats and possibly typhoid – struck me, in my dainty child-free state, as the most disgusting things I'd ever encountered.

But familiarity breeds ... if not affection, then complacency, at least. Once you've been host to them yourself a couple of times, and pulled them out of your children's hair more times than you can count, it's hard to sustain the same sense of outrage when yet another one comes along. Obviously, to have a head that's *crawling* with lice is faintly repellent. Okay, yes, it's completely revolting. Bring on the Hedrin. But the odd one or two roaming about? They don't do any harm, after all. Like the rest of us, they're only trying to eke out a little life for themselves. Poor things. Who are we to begrudge them that?

'*For there is nothing either good or bad,*' as Hamlet wisely observed, '*but thinking makes it so.*' I'm pretty sure he was referring to head lice at the time.


## School Gatherings Requiring The Presence Of Quietly Smiling Mums

No shortage of these, is there? Sometimes I wonder if they're not piled on in quite the way they are, specifically to antagonise busy mothers. But of course they aren't! On the contrary. And obviously, in principle, the more a school welcomes its parents in, the better.

That said ...

Since, for most of us, attending *all* these little events would be impossible, it makes sense, for our own peace of mind, to free ourselves from too strong a sense of obligation about any of them; and only ever attend a few and only ever as a sort of favour/kiddie treat. It's no fun, feeling like you're letting people down. Much better to lower everyone's expectations from the start.

With three children, not all at the same school, I think if I attended everything I was meant to – (haha) – all the matches, sports days, swimming contests, school fetes, concerts, plays, discussions about New Sixth Form Blocks, confabs about the food in the canteen – my life might well grind to a halt. At any rate, it would certainly feel as though it had.

Most of the time, the Lazy Mothering modus as promoted on these pages works for the greater enjoyment of both parties – mother and child – or at least not at the cost of either party, but I can't quite pull off the argument here. My children (less as they grow older, of course) would generally prefer it if I attended their school functions. Why wouldn't they?

And yet I don't ... because, as I explain to the children, *time is of the essence*. And **although I love them tenderly** there are often other things, not related to them, that I either need or would prefer to be doing.

Added to which, by the way, even if I didn't have work to do, even if I had a fleet of nannies and housekeepers and – gosh – a tax-deductable chauffeur, I would still want to limit what hours I spend, in this short life, making polite conversation on rain-soaked touchlines, or sitting in school halls watching other people's children playing musical instruments badly.

It's annoying of me. But so it goes. Children who grow up understanding that their mother's world doesn't solely revolve around theirs are much the better for it. *In my opinion.* That is to say, I think it makes them less self-centred, more self-reliant and, well, better feminists. Three qualities I happen to rate above most. Hokey Cokey? Other mothers lay greater emphasis on different human qualities, and so bring up their children differently ...

In any case, my children seem to take it on the chin. As Mick Jagger so astutely pointed out, *You can't always get what you want ...*

In the early years, before it occurred to me what a high proportion of these wretched occasions amounted to nothing much more than Stepford-style exercises in mummy-hoop-jumping, I did indeed try to participate in as many of them as possible. I attended after-drop-off, get-to-know-each-other coffee mornings, accompanied classes on trips to pantomimes and museums (okay, one pantomime, one museum). I have sat and sweated at the side of the municipal swimming baths, whooping encouragement while my children doggy-paddled from one end of a shallow end to another ... I have sold second-hand uniforms at the school fete uniform stand, and cakes at the cake stand and books at the bookstand ... and so on.

Indeed I have. It's nothing compared to the extraordinary – eccentric – levels of effort put in by some of the mothers. Nevertheless, I have done my bit. Some of it was enjoyable. Some of it was useful. Most of it was painless enough.

But all of it eats up precious *time*.

What infuriates me are those occasions when you *know* your presence is unnecessary and improves nothing for anyone, and yet still you attend: for the solitary reason that you 'feel you must', because everyone else is. Because they felt they must, too.

*But why?*

Because our children want us there.

*But why do our children want us there?*

Because ... their friends' mothers are there.

*But why are their friends' mothers there?*

Because ... Just because ... We're all there ... But nobody really knows why.

I attended a Welcome-to-Autumn-Term meeting at one or other school or nursery school, many years ago ... which ground to a halt when one of the mothers wondered how the children could be encouraged to wash their hands before and after using the fucking water fountain. So we sat on our minuscule chairs, a room full of mostly intelligent, busy women, many of whom had left work specifically to be present, while a discussion slowly unfolded and slowly went nowhere at all about the germs that might possibly lurk near water fountains in muddy playgrounds. Nobody said:

*'Come on, guys* ... this is a non-problem. *Can we move this on?'* Nobody said it. We simply sat there, politely smiling. *Just because*. That's what the other mothers did. Because that's what mothers do!

I attended another meeting in another school assembly hall, this one about the possibility of children embarking on a week-long cultural exchange with some students in China, of all magnificent adventures. I sat in that school hall for an hour, *tick-tock, tick-tock*, while the Neurotic Faction tossed in their pathetic questions ...

'What if the kids don't like the Chinese food?'

'Will the host school be providing a Western-style menu option?'

But I digress. (Only, it is staggering what some people will find to worry about, and how shameless they are about airing it, and how feeble the rest of us are, allowing them to do it on our time.)

The point is – there are many parts to family life, and I don't think it's too controversial to suggest that different mothers lay emphasis on and draw pleasure from different aspects. Some mothers genuinely enjoy going to meetings. I don't. Some mothers genuinely believe that playground hygiene around the water fountain is a valid and interesting preoccupation: something that's worth dedicating an afternoon to discussing. And although I will never understand why, I certainly don't want to prevent them from indulging that innocent pleasure. Only, please, don't make it something the rest feel obliged to listen in on.

## Distressing Cakes For The School Fair

It's the opening scene of the successful novel whose title I have parodied for this book. Isn't it? I think it is. At any rate it's the opening scene in the film – of the book – which film I couldn't get beyond the first fifteen minutes before switching off, because I simply couldn't understand what the silly woman was fussing about. What did she think she might be achieving by being such a ridiculous fraud? And why were we supposed to sympathise with her? In her desperation to conform to a set of rules she clearly didn't believe in, she only perpetuated what, it seems to me, has always been an odious and unhelpful pretence – that real mothers should feel obliged to make time for baking (which pastime has become symbolic of all good maternal virtues).

Aside from exhausting herself for no sensible reason, the 'heroine' – coward that she is – was passing on a message to her child that it's better to cringe and to lie and to do as you're told, no matter how preposterous, than to speak up for yourself and refuse to be pushed around.

Seriously. If we mothers are too lily-livered to defy convention for our own sakes then perhaps, we might do it for our daughters and save them being led the same fatuous dance twenty-five years down the road.

Next time a letter comes home asking for a home-baked cake for the cake sale, simply explain (what they all know perfectly well anyway) that you can't provide it because

You

Don't

Have

Time.

You don't feel like it ...

And because the cakes in the shop cost less and taste better anyway.


## School Fundraising

Also – actually – if you're feeling REALLY brave (count me out on this one), you might want throw in a question about what fund the cake is being baked to raise money for. It's one thing, raising money for charity – obviously. It's another thing (and this – especially, but not exclusively – applies to private schools) that we should busy ourselves raising money for an educational establishment already bleeding us dry and which, in any case, already has more than enough to be getting on with.

It's as if school fund-raising were a nervous tick, just something extra for mothers and fathers to fuss about, regardless of what funds are actually needed ... And I'm treading on dodgy ground here. I am not a teacher. What do I know about which extravagant gadgets and pieces of equipment are actually worthwhile teaching aids? Nothing much. But I remember this:

As a child, the headmistress at my village primary school waged a long crusade for the entire school to be relocated in a brand new building up the road. One day, I was lolling by the old school gate, waiting for my mother to fetch me, and overheard two other mothers discussing the campaign.

'It's disgusting,' the smaller mother said, and the other one, very tall, with long blotchy cheeks, nodded so hard her cheeks wobbled. 'In this day and age,' the little one continued, 'it's a disgrace that our kiddies have to cross the playground to get to the toilets. In the rain and the snow ...'

'In this day and age,' repeated Long-Cheeks. 'It's disgusting.'

And I remember gazing from one to the other, wondering what they were fussing about. What was so 'disgusting' about crossing the playground? I didn't mind crossing the playground. It hadn't occurred to me to mind. It was just something you did if you wanted to get to the toilet.

Anyway, God knows how many busy-mum fundraisers (and tax-payers' pounds) later, the will of the headmistress finally prevailed. The school was given a spanking new building up the road and we didn't have to cross the playground to go to the toilet any more. AND, by the way, that was a shame. Because as a child, it's quite fun to cross the playground from time to time.

Schools – private and state – seem to get a bit hung up on student comfort and equipment, and honestly, I can't be *the only* parent who doesn't care, who positively prefers it, actually, if the children have sometimes to 'mend and make do' (as they said in the olden days). Necessity is the mother of invention – and all that. As long as a school has the essentials – intelligent, kind, imaginative teachers, and enough space and – I'll stop there. I am not a teacher. I won't presume to list what constitutes the 'essentials'.

But. If I were ever going to bake a cake for a fundraiser (which is unlikely), it would need to be for a decent cause; a local hospice, let's say. Something valid. And not so my precious kiddies can have a machine for bowling cricket balls let's say. And certainly not so they enjoy uninterrupted central heating en route to going to the toilet.

## Watching Children Enjoying Their Hobbies

Like a lot of boys my son loves football. I am proud of his dedication and skill, and delighted by his passion. My youngest daughter, meanwhile, loves colouring in, baking inedible biscuits and bouncing interestingly on trampolines. My eldest daughter enjoys all sorts of things: among them writing plays and playing tennis and making subtly delicious toasted sandwiches. ALL THIS IS GOOD.

Having hobbies is good.

But I don't think they need endless parental validation before they can be considered a pleasure. Parents don't need to stand by and watch. Far better, I would have thought, that they get a life – and find some hobbies of their own.

If a child develops a passion for pottery, let's say, there may sometimes be a nice pot to be rejoiced over along the way. And an enthusiastic mother, on spotting Excellent Pottery Promise in her offspring, might take care to provide said offspring with – I don't know, access to a kiln. But is she also required to sit around, life on hold, and watch while he or she models the clay? I think not. By the same token, nor do I feel duty-bound to watch my children playing their weekly sports matches. Any more than I would expect even the most ardent of admirers to watch and applaud, in the cold and the rain, while I sat reading *Private Eye*.

Sport is not a performance art. Lots of people enjoy watching it – yes – (not me) but that's not its *raison d'être*. Its *raison d'être* is in the taking part.

And it's a symptom of our neurotic meddlesomeness; our overblown belief in our own importance as parents, along with a lack of faith in our children's ability to enjoy life, independent of our active approval, that sends us out there to the touchlines, week after ice-cold week, to watch and clap and shout while our child … *has fun*. Why bother? Why not find our own fun? Our children will have plenty enough fun without us standing there. Possibly (dare I suggest?)

without us breathing down their necks, they might even have more.

## Boredom

When I was a child it was a major ingredient of every weekend and school holiday. So much so, I invented a song. I would lie on my bed with my feet resting against the wall and sing it on a single note, for surprisingly long stretches:

Bor-ing
Bor-ing
What shall we do?
Typhoo
Boring

It killed hours – days probably – if you totted them up. Eventually the sheer b-o-r-e-d-o-m of the song would drive me, half-zombified, to do something else. And, in desultory fashion, I would find another way to not-quite-amuse myself, until the next option presented itself. Boredom, as much as necessity, was ever the mother of invention. Not everything invented has to be worthwhile.

Boredom is part of childhood. Actually – it's part of life. Learning to cope with it is one of the great requirements of adulthood. So it's a mystery why we – modern parents – go to such neurotic lengths to banish it from our children's lives.

Sometimes just sitting and thinking is good.

## *After-School Activities And School Holidays*

My heart used to sink when I returned home to find the children flopped in front of the Wii – or in front of any screen, come to that. Life is so short, I would think frantically, and it's not even raining outside! They should be *doing* something, learning something, being stimulated, acquiring skills! And yet here they are, cooped up in an overheated sitting room, possibly without having bothered to switch the lights on, the haze of inertia so thick around them it almost gleams.

Of all the aspects of child-rearing, it's the one, I think, which, in the early years, tormented me most. The tidal wave of guilt that hit me each time I returned from work to see my children looking listless and bored; and hit me again with double the force, each time one of the Supermothers sent one of their bloody round robins, suggesting yet more jolly Day Camps, Fun Days, or after-school hobbies – every one of which cost money, every one of which required transport to and from ...

Children have so much free time. The school holidays are so long. We can't provide them with entertainment each and every day. Practically and financially (for me at least), it is an impossibility. *What are we to do with them, then?*

It was one of the reasons the family moved out of the city – however briefly. The guilt, m'lud. *The guilt!* I fondly imagined, with all those fields outside, that the problem of Amusing The Children, in a wholesome and possibly even educational manner, would be cheaply and easily resolved. I listened to the propaganda that dribbled from the mouths of the evacuees, those former urbanites who had decamped to the country before us. (Most of whom, I've since discovered, spend their waking hours behind the wheel of a car, driving children to school and back, to discos and back and to trampoline clubs and tap dance classes ...) 'Oh we just open the back door,' they said smugly, 'and we bung the kids outside and we don't see them again until teatime!' Stupidly (bearing in mind I grew up in the country myself) or perhaps, out of sheer, blind desperation, I believed them.

I remember, a month or two after we had moved to the country, urging my daughter, then seven, to switch off the telly and go outside and play. She said, 'Trouble is, though, it turns out fields are quite boring.'

I had fields galore where I grew up. And they weren't always boring. Obviously. But they often were. For my generation, boredom, as I said, was part of life.

And maybe it's because childish boredom can be so easily and immediately resolved today – just open the door, bung them in front of a screen and you won't hear from them again until teatime/tomorrow/next year – that we tend to feel so uncomfortable with it.

In any case – country life didn't solve anything. Same screens. Same inertia.

We returned to London, and the question of how-to-amuse-the-children remained as desperate as ever ... the situation was out of control. Between them they were attending trampoline camps and drama lessons, football coaching and street dance classes, modern dance lessons, ballet classes, and swimming classes, stand-up comedy tuition (I exaggerate not) ... and though, in truth, it was remarkably little compared with the after-school activities of many of their friends, it was more than I could afford. Finally, thankfully, came the extra-curricular extravagance that broke the camel's back, and which gave me the courage to dump the lot of them. (Well, okay ... Most.)

## The Epiphany

There are a couple of tennis courts quite near to our house, which the children are allowed to play on. At the far end of one of them there is also a wall, which means if they can't find another human to play tennis with, they can always play against that.

One of my fellow school mothers – clever and likeable in all respects, guilty about having to work through her children's holidays, neurotic about her child spending any time not gainfully designated – emailed to say she had found a tennis coach. She had three other children lined up to share the lesson, and wondered if my child wanted to be the fourth. The cost could then be divided between the four children. Clearly. She said she haggled the price down – and I'm sure she had. Nevertheless, it still cost money which, not only did I not want to spend on tennis coaching, I didn't want to have to remember to have in my purse, to hand to my child, to hand to the coach on the right morning of the right day each week.

For a tennis lesson which, frankly, my child could easily do without.

I ignored the email (often the best response of course when you want something to go away) and several other emails that followed, but then, as luck would have it, I bumped into her in person.

She said, 'Oooh I've been wanting to talk to you.'

*Bollocks.*

She presented her case. To which I replied, 'I can't really afford it.'

This statement can embarrass people, especially if they are noticeably richer than you are. In general, it's an excellent line to drop, if you're not brave enough to say:

• 'It's just that I'd prefer to spend the cash on something else.'
OR
• 'Hmm. All sounds a bit hassly. Not sure I can be shagged.'

(Both of which, in this instance – I'll be honest – would have been closer to the truth.)

She was quite embarrassed. Because she is a nice woman. And because she is noticeably richer than I am. She said, *'But if we divide the cost by four* ... And if we pay for five or ten lessons in advance ...'

To which I replied, 'In any case, there's a tennis court just sitting there. Why can't they just hit against each other?'

She looked taken aback. She said, 'Well—' (I don't think

the question had even occurred to her). 'They'd only muck about ...'

'Not if they want to play tennis, they won't muck about,' I replied.

'And if they *don't* want to play tennis, so what? I don't care if they muck about. As long as I'm not paying for it. Do you?'

If I'd been speaking Japanese I think she might have understood me better. She wandered away looking slightly shell-shocked, and I wondered if I had been rude.

Still do wonder, actually. Hope not.

Either way, it was the end of the discussion. And the beginning of a new extra-curricular-free life.

It so happens, at the end of a long and boring day, my children can often be found banging a tennis ball listlessly against that tennis court wall. Or not. Sometimes they're lolling against that tennis court wall, chatting. Or lying on the tarmac, staring at the clouds. Or lying on the tarmac, squabbling.

It doesn't cost a thing. It's another way of passing the time. Or, at least, another location to pass it in. And it's within walking distance of home.

That'll do.

We adults harp on about the magic of childhood as if we'd stumbled on a new religion. But a part of the magic (which often drives parents to distraction) is the childish lack of hurry; the liberated sense that to waste an hour staring at the clouds matters not a whit, because there are *infinite* hours where that one came from still ...

Children have all the time in the world. Lucky things. So what if they spend vast tracks of it simply gestating? (Previously known as 'relaxing'.) I only wish I could learn from them, and remember how do it half so well myself.

Computer games are a waste of time. We know that. Lying on the sofa staring at the ceiling is a waste of time. Spending all morning in bed … Watching *Harry Potter and the Order of the Phoenix* for the 30,987th time … in due course, children will grow out of their inertia – and they will start racing around with fraught, grey scowls on their faces, dividing their days into dismal little units of TO-DO … just like their parents. In the meantime let us save ourselves the money, the petrol, the time and energy, the guilt, the sheer boredom of having to organise alternatives, and leave them in peace to do what they really want to do: as often as not, absolutely nothing at all.

**P.S.** Also, (by the way) there's something a bit pathetic about children who need to be spoon-fed adult-approved amusement every moment of the day. Isn't there? Don't they have any resources of their own, for God's sake? No spirit of adventure? No desire for privacy or independence, or rebellion? *Anything?* Useless little sods.

But moving on.

## The Magic Of Childhood

Those four words together conjure up something golden-lit: perhaps a John Lewis ad in the run-up to Christmas; or a supermarket ad for Christmas. Supermarkets always love a Magic of Childhood Christmas theme. There's handsome Dad driving through the snow, and a smiling wife and a real log fire and an amazingly well-baubled tree – and there'll be food enough to feed the 5,000, laid out and glistening on platters. And a couple of bouncing, shiny kids in clean pyjamas, and lots and lots of symmetrically wrapped presents ...

The Magic of Childhood! Presents are certainly part of it (no arguing with that). As indeed are Christmas trees and happy homes and clean pyjamas. And that sense of the absolute, locked-out security – which those ads portray so well – and which children can feel sometimes, in the bosom of their family.

Sadly, in our desperation to capture, style, package, share and – above all – render *safe*, the magic we all remember so fondly, I think we sometimes end up doing the opposite. We spend fortunes, we bend over backwards, we fly our children to Euro Disney, and take family breaks to *Lapland* ... (words fail me). But so much adult interference, so much purpose-specific kit, so much pre-planning and pre-sanitising perfection ... makes it all the harder to be lost in an experience. With all our good will and worn-out wallets, I wonder if we don't only succeed in sucking the magic out of everything.

Certainly, I know all my most magical, happiest childhood memories (aside from the opening of presents, obviously) involved adventures – voyages of danger and discovery – not with adults and their interminable don'ts-and-be-carefuls tagging needlessly along; but with other children, as wide-eyed, excited and fearful as I was.

The real magic of childhood is an open, childish mind – and a free spirit. Both of which are better accessed when the adults butt out, find their own amusements, and leave the children in peace to enjoy their childish fun alone.

# Christmas Eve

*It's the end of the day ... the end of the year ... it's Christmas Eve.*

And as I write these last few words I realise there's a faint danger, on their publication, that the social workers may come knocking – and the police – and the midwives too; and the kiddie psychologists, the road safety experts ... and the Supermums, the Mumgelicals, the Orgasimums and the Catholics ... And the health visitors ... and the doctors and the sports teachers ... and the makers of television commercials ... and the Wet Dads and the cuckolded dads, and the cheated wives and the stay-at-home-mums, and the *mums who DON'T CARE about what they gave up and instead, LOVE what they got in return* ... In fact, only thinking about all the people who might want to come knocking ... makes me want to retire to my room for a good long nap, and only wake up when they promise they've found something else to disapprove of.

Fact is, I wouldn't have dared to write it when the children were still babies – for fear of all the things we all fear: all the things that might have gone wrong. But they didn't go wrong, did they? Despite all the short cuts, the wanton selfishness of this loving MUM, here I am with two children almost grown and a third with her babyhood far behind her. Three healthy children who, despite their shamelessly un-Supermother, are *doing just fine.* Or better than fine, actually. Much, much *much* better than fine, if you ask me. But then again, I am their mother.

As I tap out these final words – at the kitchen table, because the central heating seems to have gone on the blink and the rest of the house is freezing – all three of them are within eyeshot.

My oldest daughter, 15, is stretched out like long, thin spaghetti on a sofa in the far corner, teeth covered in superglue, she says, having tried and failed to fix her own orthodontic brace. (There's no way round it: I suppose we shall have to make an appointment.) She is watching a DVD of the French movie, *Subway*, in search of the exact quote you will have read, on page 194. The task defeated me. (The film hasn't aged well.) So I've bribed her to watch it for me. I thought £4 was more than generous, with a tea and biscuit service thrown in. But she must have smelled my desperation because somehow she's haggled me up to an astronomical £7.75.

My son, 12, is playing keepy-uppy right here beside me – beside my laptop more to the point (it's making me nervous), and talking to me as I write. He's talking ludicrously fast. *Bounce-bounce* ... Saying something about a *one-touch dummy run* ... something ... *back-heeling a corner kick to the far post* ... and a referee ... and God only knows if he's talking about a game he actually played, or something that happened between Chelsea and – oh, Sunderland? It doesn't matter. He knows I'm not listening. It's part of his private joke. He's killing time until Christmas begins, demonstrating his freakish ability to say very, very dull things, very, very quickly (while playing keepy-uppy) ... until the sheer idiocy – and the volume – threaten to kill me with boredom and I beg him to stop. I'm laughing as I write this ... but in a moment we both know I will break.

The six-year-old is in the hall, her father's laptop on the floor in front of her, teaching herself the dance steps to a new Olly Murs video she's found on YouTube. There's a lot of hip jiving going on: outrageous levels of hip jiving, in fact. I've just told her she was dancing like a slapper – and it's hard to tell if she knows what a slapper is. But I think she got the gist. Laughed like a drain and hip jived even harder.

So there you have it. My magical children. Or magical to me, at any rate. Funny. Resourceful. Excellent company. And happy, I think. For the moment, anyway ... I am more proud of them than it is possible to say.

*It's the end of the day ... the end of the year ... it's Christmas Eve ...* As I write these last few words I must admit I am not entirely certain where their magical father may be. It's the party season, after all. If he ever told me where he was going, I probably wasn't listening. Tonight, in any case, at some point soon, we'll all be back sharing the same house again. We shall be hanging out our magical children's ridiculous Christmas stockings, the contents of which, fresh from the pound shops of Hammersmith, are lying in a scrappy heap on our bedroom floor, awaiting our soon-to-be-drunken attention.

Yes, the sun could be shining. We could be in the Caribbean. We might have won the lottery. My daughter's teeth might not be covered in superglue ... our heads might be nit-free zones ... and all that ... I might have sworn a little less ...

My workaholic husband might have been around a little more ... the central heating might be working ... But aside from that (what have the Romans ever done for us?), we seem to be in pretty good shape. There are no martyrs among us. And no victims. Just five individuals, hungry for life, who love each other, care for each other and respect each other; who enjoy each other's company (on the whole) and who are very much looking forward to Christmas. Tomorrow the cousinly hordes will gather. And that'll be fun. But tonight it's just us. And a Chinese takeaway. Who knows what lies ahead? But at this moment at least, I don't believe family life could be any better.

*They fuck you up, your mum [and dad] ...*

And one way or another, no matter what we do or don't do, I dare say we always will. But with a little less fussing and tutting we might at least have a merrier time of it in the process ...

# Acknowledgements

Thanks to my girlfriends for sharing their irritations and frustrations with our soppy status quo, and for feeding the furnace with some excellent horror stories.

Apologies to anyone or anything – any institution, friend, neighbour or random individual who believes they may recognise themselves in these pages. Chillax! You do not! You CAN not! I super-slyly disguised you all.

Thank you Clare Alexander, Amanda Harris, Jillian Young, Jessica Gulliver ...

And above all, obviously, thank you to my children. For being perfect.

Amen.

W&N
*blog and newsletter*

For literary discussion, author insight,
book news, exclusive content,
recipes and giveaways, visit the
Weidenfeld & Nicolson blog and
sign up for the newsletter at:

## www.wnblog.co.uk

For breaking news, reviews and exclusive competitions
Follow us 🐦 @wnbooks
Find us 📘 facebook.com/WNfiction